ENCOUNTER
SERIES

American Apostasy: The Triumph of "Other" Gospels

Essays by

Peter L. Berger
Avery Dulles, S.J.
Robert W. Jenson
James Turner

and
The Story of an Encounter by
Paul T. Stallsworth

Edited and with a Foreword by
Richard John Neuhaus

WILLIAM B. EERDMANS PUBLISHING COMPANY
GRAND RAPIDS, MICHIGAN

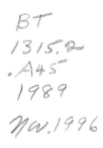

Published by Wm. B. Eerdmans Publishing Co.
in cooperation with
The Rockford Institute Center on Religion & Society

Copyright © 1989 by Wm. B. Eerdmans Publishing Co.
255 Jefferson Ave. S.E., Grand Rapids, Mich. 49503

Library of Congress Cataloging-in-Publication Data

American apostasy: the triumph of "other" gospels /
  essays by Peter L. Berger . . . [et al.] and The story of an encounter
  by Paul T. Stallsworth; edited and with a foreword
  by Richard John Neuhaus.
      p.   cm.   —(Encounter series; 10)
   Contents: Different Gospels / Peter L. Berger—Secular justification
of truth claims / James Turner—Gospel, church, and politics /
Avery Dulles—A protestant constructive response to Christian
unbelief / Robert W. Jenson—The story of an encounter /
Paul T. Stallsworth.
   ISBN 0-8028-0210-9
   1. Apostasy—Congresses. I. Berger, Peter L. II. Neuhaus, Richard
John.   III. Series: Encounter series (Grand Rapids, Mich.); 10.
BT1315.2.A45   1989
273.9—dc19   88-30148
                                                           CIP

Contents

Foreword

The claim that our churches today—across the denominational board—have fallen into apostasy is a heavy charge. It is the charge brought by Peter Berger, widely recognized as America's foremost sociologist of religion, in the Erasmus Lecture published here. Berger speaks both as a social scientist and as a Christian believer. In the former capacity, he offers an analysis of "the new knowledge class" in American religion, an analysis that has already come in for a great deal of lively discussion. As a committed Christian, Berger defines the gospel from which the churches have apostasized in a way that some participants in this conference thought altogether too Lutheran. As the reader will see, however, all participants agree that, by whatever definition, apostasy from the gospel is an issue as urgent today as it was when Paul wrote to the Galatians.

Christians in the Reformation traditions have customarily said that the church is always in need of reformation. Since the Second Vatican Council, Roman Catholics have regularly said that as well. But the general proposition that the church is always in need of reformation can become routine, and the sense of urgency be lost. When the language of "crisis" is thrown at thoughtful people from every direction, they tend to become skeptical. That said, this book is nonetheless premised upon a recognition of crisis—*the* crisis of whether much of the church has abandoned the gospel and therefore ceased to be church. The people in this book believe that it is not only legitimate but imperative to ask whether this has happened. Believing that, they are prepared to run the risk of historical pretension in urging a New Reformation. In sum, this is not simply another academic conference. It is an earnest wrestling with the future of Christianity in the world.

Historian James Turner reminds us, as historians are wont to do, that our situation is not utterly singular. He makes it clear, however, that parallels with other times in no way diminish the newness and the seriousness of our moment. In an argument that is as complex as it is rewarding, Robert Jenson contends that the crisis is in the most precise sense theological—that is, it is a crisis in our Christian understanding of God, Father, Son, and Holy Spirit. Avery Dulles's paper, which has already received considerable attention in the general and religious press, focuses, appropriately, on the Roman Catholic situation. He offers a profound insight into Roman Catholic anxieties about the new prominence given to political pronouncements, as in the case of the bishops' letters on nuclear war and economics. The reader is invited to ask, with Dulles, discomfiting questions about the response to the bishops' initiatives. If, as the bishops assert, their sociopolitical positions are drawn from the wells of Catholic tradition, why is it that their positions are so warmly applauded by those who care nothing about that tradition and so hesitantly received by many who both understand and love that tradition? Father Dulles, as any fair-minded reader will recognize, is not condemning but exploring; he is trying to understand what has gone wrong—and what has gone right—in the ways that the Roman Catholic Church is attempting to speak the gospel to the world. Among the questions raised by Dulles is whether Christians today have the nerve to sustain a community with a peculiar language of faith or whether, in the name of "translating" and "applying" the tradition, we are abandoning the community, the language, and the faith itself.

The participants did not all agree on the meaning of apostasy, although they did agree on the importance of finding out what apostasy might mean in our time. Some insisted that it is not so much a matter of abandoning the gospel as it is of permitting the gospel to be displaced or eclipsed by other gospels. Others thought such distinctions altogether too fine. David Lotz, church historian at Union Theological Seminary in New York, argues that *the* gospel has become but one option among the many gospels proclaimed by the contemporary church. We are awash in gospels, he says. "There are gospels everywhere." And, he adds, in centers of "liberalism" such as Union all kinds of new orthodoxies are rigidly enforced. It is as G. K. Chesterton said about believing in God: the problem with people who stop believing in God is not that they end up believing in nothing but that they end up believing in anything.

In the final session, Carl Braaten of the Lutheran School of Theology at Chicago summed up the conclusion of many. He asserted that theological education today has abdicated its responsibility to teach theology. In the "academic model" of theological education, said Braaten, we do not teach theology: we teach *about* theology, and mainly we teach about theologians. Seldom does the professor put his own profession/confession "on the line." Academic disengagement and a false "objectivity" provide the pattern in much that is called theological education, and this too is a kind of apostasy, said Braaten, speaking for others as well. The painful possibility is posed that both church seminaries and university divinity schools have now trained several generations of ministers in the promulgation of apostasy. Nor is it to be thought that evangelicals are exempt from the pattern here analyzed. Outside of the theological "mainstream" for a long time, many evangelicals are now boasting, in effect, that they are academically certified to be as apostate as anybody else. With a great release of long-pent-up energy, much of evangelicalism has brought new enthusiasm to the Gadarene sweepstakes of contemporary theology.

This is, all in all, a provocative and disturbing book. My own feeling is that toward the end we were moving too quickly toward answers and remedies. Maybe we should have stayed longer with trying to understand the nature of the crisis and with letting its implications sink in. And maybe not. In any event, you can judge for yourself. There is one judgment that I am sure you will come to: if there is any merit at all in the analysis of apostasy offered here, there is no pretension at all in speaking of the need for a New Reformation. As several participants noted, and as all participants agreed, such a Reformation will be the product not of our planning but of the Spirit's renewal of a community pledged to no other gospel.

THE ROCKFORD INSTITUTE   Richard John Neuhaus
CENTER ON RELIGION & SOCIETY
NEW YORK CITY

ACKNOWLEDGMENTS: We are grateful to the Pew Charitable Trusts for funding the conference that produced this book. And I am, as always, personally indebted to my colleagues Allan Carlson, Paul Stallsworth, and Davida Goldman for their generosity and good spirit in attending to the innumerable tasks that sustain the work of the Center on Religion & Society.   —RJN

Different Gospels:
The Social Sources of Apostasy

Peter L. Berger

The Apostle Paul wrote to the Galatians as follows:

> I am astonished that you are so quickly deserting him who
> called you in the grace of Christ and turning to a different
> gospel—not that there is another gospel, but there are some
> who trouble you and want to pervert the gospel of Christ. . . .
> As we have said before, so now I say again, If any one is preach-
> ing to you a gospel contrary to that which you received, let him
> be accursed. (Gal. 1:6-7, 9, RSV)

This is not a sermon. It is, as advertised, a lecture.* A sermon is an
act of proclamation of the gospel by an individual who has been ordained to preach. That is a very solemn business indeed, one to
which I have neither claim nor aspiration. I am not a preacher; I am
a social scientist. I exercise a vocation that deals not in proclamation
but in empirical inquiry, which by its very nature is tentative, prob-
abilistic, and open to falsification. Most of what I have to say in this
lecture is based on my observations as a sociologist with an interest
in American religion. I see no reason, however, to limit myself to
doing sociology of religion. I am also a Christian. As such I find
myself constrained to relate my understanding of the world to my
faith, and I will attempt to do this in the latter part of the lecture. It
is with this intention, and definitely not to suggest a sermon, that I
begin with a passage from the New Testament.

The theme of this passage is apostasy. People, especially those of
a conservative bent, have the tendency to think that their own age
has unique evils. To some extent, I suppose, this is a correct perception. Every age has a distinctive genius, for evil as well as good, and
our age has produced evils that can safely be called unique. But

---

*This Erasmus lecture was delivered by Dr. Berger 22 January 1987 at
St. Peter's Lutheran Church in New York City.

1

apostasy—the substitution of different gospels for the gospel of Christ—has been a constant in the history of the church. It was there right from the beginning, as the letter to the Galatians (along with many other portions of the New Testament) serves to remind us. The essence of apostasy is always the same: seeking salvation not in the grace of Christ "heard with faith" but rather in what Paul calls "the works of the law." The specific contents of apostasy, the details of "works righteousness," vary from age to age. This lecture is a reflection about apostasy in our own age. As a social scientist I have certain analytic tools allowing an attempt to understand the mundane context of the "different gospels" of the age. As a Christian I must also make some moral and theological assessments.

Let us do some sociology.

For historically well-known reasons (elaborated by, among others, H. Richard Niebuhr in the book whose title I have paraphrased here), there has always been a close linkage between religion and culture in America. This is a culture whose values and institutions, even whose aesthetic style, have been crucially affected by Protestantism. Thus there is a direct line from the Puritan covenant, through the "half-way covenants" of a disintegrating Puritanism, to the various secularized notions of American exceptionalism—all having in common the idea that, somehow, American society has a unique and putatively sacred mission. To be sure, there have been dissenters from this vision (within Protestantism and from without), and some American groups have never shared it. But its pervasiveness in American history to this day is remarkable, especially in comparison with societies having a more sober conception of themselves. In due course Catholics, Jews, and others have come to participate in this quasicovenantal vision, but, not surprisingly, the major Protestant denominations have had the most intimate connection with the culture. American civilization is a distinctively Protestant product; conversely, American Protestantism is a distinctively powerful example of so-called *Kulturprotestantismus*.

Sociologically, however, one can describe this religiocultural unity more precisely. Here again Richard Niebuhr (building to some extent on Max Weber) is helpful: it is not culture in general that has been the partner in this marriage with religion; it is a specific *class* culture. The class, of course, is the bourgeoisie, lately called the middle class, that creator and carrier of capitalism which had to struggle against older classes in Europe but which had hardly any serious competitors in America (except in the antebellum South, though even that is debatable). America, from the beginning, was a bour-

geois society—not, of course, in the sense that all Americans were middle-class but because this society was shaped by middle-class values and institutions without having to overcome antecedent aristocratic or peasant cultures. As both Weber and Niebuhr showed, Protestant morality and Protestant social arrangements were highly instrumental in the construction of this bourgeois world. Protestantism not only inspired the culture of the great American middle class, but it served as the very effective mobility machine by which people from the lower reaches of society, generation after generation, were assisted in *moving into* the middle class. Religiously (and, of course, sincerely so) lower-class individuals were washed in the blood of the Lamb in one great revival after another. But in the process they also learned to wash their feet and to wash out their mouths—that is, to act and speak in accordance with middle-class norms, and ipso facto to acquire habits and attitudes conducive to upward mobility in a relatively open class system. Already John Wesley observed (and was troubled by) the fact that Methodists had a pronounced tendency to start out poor and end up rich; Weber and Niebuhr would have had no difficulty explaining to him why this was happening.

As recently as the 1950s this class-specific "culture Protestantism" was very much alive and well. The so-called mainline denominations existed in a by-and-large happy symbiosis with middle-class culture; lower-class sects and churches were continuing to grind away their time-honored mobility machinery; and (as Will Herberg astutely observed at the time) Catholics and Jews had very largely joined this all-American celebration. To be sure, there had been a good deal of secularization in the content of this common American faith, both in its social and its personal ethics (President Eisenhower embodied the former modification, Norman Vincent Peale the latter), and many of the harder theological contents of the various traditions had been softened, relativized (or, as John Murray Cuddihy has put it, "civilized"). The main point, though, is that there was little tension between the major religious groupings and the cultural milieu in which they found themselves. They existed (if I may use a term I employed in my first writings about American religion) in an "okay world": America was okay; the middle-class way of life was okay; indeed, it had become difficult to distinguish between the religiously sanctioned virtues and the values propagated by politicians, civics teachers, and therapists. If I'm to recall one *locus classicus* in the portrayal of this religiocultural symbiosis (a critical one, of course), it would be William Lee Miller's "Piety along the Potomac" (published in *The Reporter* magazine in 1954); his essay

"The Gospel of Norman Vincent Peale" (*Union Seminary Quarterly Review*, 1955) would round out the picture in its more personal aspect.

Looking back on this period thirty years later, one can easily say that the situation today is very different. And so it is, in many respects. But it is for that reason all the more important to understand that in other respects the situation hasn't changed that much.

I would argue that one of the most important developments of the post–World War II period in America (and incidentally in other Western societies) has been *a bifurcation of the middle class*. This is the so-called "New Class thesis," an idea that, interestingly, has been held in common by observers on the right and the left of the political spectrum. Thus both Irving Kristol, the doyen of neoconservatism, and Alvin Gouldner, the late neo-Marxist sociologist, have both written about the "New Class," pretty much agreeing on its empirical characteristics. Kristol thinks that this class is bad news, while Gouldner hoped that it would bring about very desirable changes in the society. When observers with diametrically opposed ideological views agree on an empirical assessment, this gives good grounds for surmising that the assessment is close to reality. What is the reality in this case?

The underlying process is technological and economic: in our type of advanced industrial society, an ever-shrinking segment of the labor force is needed to keep material production going. This frees up—indeed compels—the growth of an occupational sector that is geared to miscellaneous services (economists call this the "quaternary sector"). Within this sector there is what has been called the "knowledge industry," and within *that* there is a very peculiar activity, devoted to the production and distribution of what may be called symbolic knowledge. The "New Class" consists of the people who make their living from this activity. These are the educators (from preschool to university), the "communicators" (in the media, in public relations, and in a miscellany of propagandistic lobbies), the therapists of all descriptions (from child analysts to geriatric sex counselors), and, last but not least, substantial elements of the bureaucracy (those elements concerned with what may be called "lifestyle engineering") and the legal profession. They are, of course, a minority of the working population, but because of their power in key institutions providing the symbols by which society understands itself, their influence is much greater than would be supposed by their numbers. Whether one calls this group a "class" or not is a matter of sociological conceptualization; I use the term because I think it helps to clarify what is going on.

It is a class because it is a group with a distinctive relation to what Marx called the "mode of production." It is a *rising* class, and as such it finds itself in conflict with the class that previously controlled the societal areas into which it is moving. That class, of course, is the *old* middle class, still centered in the business community and the traditional professions. The conflict between the two middle classes, I believe, serves to explain many otherwise strange features of recent American politics—notably the fact that many economically and culturally privileged people have moved into strong, sometimes virulent opposition to key American institutions and values. The new knowledge class is generally left of center. This fact, I think, can very largely be explained by the vested interests of this class, which, to put it very broadly, stands to gain from a shift of power from business to government. Thus this class has a vested interest in domestic policies that expand the welfare state and in foreign policies that deemphasize military power. I regret that I cannot elaborate on this assertion here, but, be this as it may, the most relevant point to be made here is that the new class (like all classes, of course) has distinctive cultural characteristics. Again, I would argue that many of the sociocultural conflicts today, from those centering on the environment to the sphere of sexual intimacy, must be understood as symbolic expressions of an underlying class conflict. Thus we know that class is the most reliable predictor of an individual's stand on such matters as nuclear energy, abortion, and the gamut of items on the feminist agenda. By their bumper stickers you shall know them: it is not difficult to guess the class affiliation of individuals whose automobiles sport such messages as "U.S. out of Central America," "Save the Whales," or "ERA Now," as against "Nicaragua Is Spanish for Afghanistan," "Register Criminals, Not Guns," or "Abortion Is Murder." The former, of course, is likely to be a fully accredited member of the new knowledge class; the latter may be an unrepentant bourgeois, or he or she may belong to that working class which (contrary to all Marxist theories) is now one of the staunchest carriers of traditional bourgeois culture.

The religious fallout of this *Kulturkampf* is all too visible. The mainline Protestant denominations still contain old-middle-class and working-class individuals (their numbers probably dwindling). But (and this is a decisively important fact) their clergy, officials, and intellectuals have (understandably enough) identified almost completely with the culture and ipso facto the political agenda of the new middle class. A very similar process has been underway in the Roman Catholic community. Contrary to what was predicted by Jeffrey Hadden in his still-interesting book *The Gathering Storm in the*

Churches (1969), laypeople who dislike the new-class rhetoric assailing them in these churches have put up remarkably little resistance; instead, they have quietly moved out. Some have joined the ranks of the unchurched; others have helped to swell the impressive numbers making up the great evangelical upsurge. And the latter too makes much more sense in the light of class analysis: to a large extent it may be seen as part of the "bourgeois insurgency" (to use Richard Neuhaus's apt phrase), which is the movement of resistance by the old middle class and much of the working class against the political and cultural power grab of the new class. In this perspective, the New Christian Right is the mirror image of the mainline leadership in the ongoing class conflict.

What I'm saying here is that, appearances notwithstanding, there has been no basic change in the relations between religion and culture or between religion and class in America. What *has* changed is the class system and its cultures. But, as always, most of American religion (and especially Protestantism) faithfully reflects the class culture in which it finds itself. As before, there is very little consciousness of the class location of one's own cultural and ideological propensities. *Kulturprotestantismus* prevails, eagerly emulated by many non- (or should one say neo-) Protestants. American society continues to be pluralistic and broadly tolerant, and one should not overestimate the degree of polarization. There are many people and entire groups who manage to live quite comfortably detached from all this political and cultural conflict. All the same, there are two class armies arrayed against each other on a sizable number of cultural battlefields. Increasingly, major religious organizations are serving the function of military chaplaincies in these armies, doing what chaplains have always done on battlefields—solemnly blessing the banners of their side and assuring the troops that their cause is God's.

Mainline Protestantism has suffered a good measure of decline. The aforementioned class conflict will largely determine whether this decline will continue. I would not want to make predictions here, but one point should be made: if the mainline churches continue to decline, it will *not* be because of their alleged "prophetic ministry." It is hardly "prophecy" if one says exactly what people in a particular social milieu want to hear. The decline will not be the result of "speaking truth to power" but rather of backing the wrong horse in a game of power politics.

Needless to say, this sociological analysis could be greatly refined and elaborated. Of necessity, I have been exceedingly sketchy here.

I would strongly emphasize, however, that the analysis is "value-neutral." *All* religious and moral affirmations occur in a social context; to point out what this context is by no means prejudges the validity of the affirmations. I, for one, find myself unable to identify fully with the agenda of either side in the current conflict. Still, *morally speaking* (and leaving aside both cultural tastes and theological convictions), I find the new-class agenda the more reprehensible of the two. It seems to me that the most pressing moral issues of the present age are the avoidance of nuclear war, the survival of freedom, and the alleviation of misery. These goals, I believe, depend upon the maintenance of a balance of power based on American military strength and upon the institutions of democratic capitalism; I further believe that the much-maligned bourgeois culture, albeit modified, continues to be a better vehicle for sustaining a decent society than its current competitors. Therefore, if pushed to make a moral choice between the "bourgeois insurgency" and the new-class agenda, I would opt for the former (though I would want to dissent from some planks of the platform). Put simply, I fail to see the moral superiority of an ideology committed to unilateral disarmament, a vague socialism, and an assault on the family. I have elsewhere written at length about my reasons for this moral position and for the right-of-center politics that follows from it. That, however, is not my purpose here. I mention it for two reasons. First, I will in what follows maintain that, in making a theological assessment, one can say the same things about those who would make a "gospel" of a right-wing agenda and those who do this with an agenda of the left—though by this I'm *not* suggesting a symmetrical *moral* equivalence. And second, I want to make my own political position clear precisely because what I have to say theologically is metapolitical; indeed, I would say *exactly the same*, speaking theologically, if I located myself on the other side of the political divide.

Paul wrote to the Galatians,

> A man is not justified by works of the law but through faith in Jesus Christ. Even we have believed in Christ Jesus, in order to be justified by faith in Christ, and not by works of the law, because by works of the law shall no one be justified. (Gal. 2:16)

Let us now do some theology. (For those of us who are not theologians, the warrant for doing this lies in the priesthood of all believers. Or, to put it in more mundane terms, theology is too important to be left to the professional theologians—especially seeing what they have done with the business of theologizing in recent years!)

Faith in the gospel of Christ is constitutive of the church. The church is the community that embodies this faith. Apostasy occurs when any other content is deemed to be constitutive of the Christian community. At that point, the community becomes something other than the church of Christ. Of all the so-called "marks of the church," the central and indispensable one is that the church proclaims the gospel and not any other message of salvation. Compared to the true gospel, all these other messages appear as "works of the law," as manifestations of "works righteousness." These allegedly salvific messages, of course, differ greatly in different periods of history. It requires a considerable effort on our part to enter into the dispute over the status of Jewish law in the Galatian community; however important one may deem the dialogue between Judaism and Christianity in our own time, I think it's safe to say that it will have to be couched in very different language in our day than it was in Paul's day and that the specific problem of the Galatians is not our problem today. The underlying question, though, has not changed at all: Is it the gospel of Christ that constitutes the church, or is it a "different gospel"?

It seems to me that we face precisely this question in American Christianity today—nothing less—and it is an awesome question. Compared to this question, the different moral and political options available to us pale not into insignificance (because Christians are in the world and responsible for the world) but into what Dietrich Bonhoeffer called "penultimacy": the ultimate question is the question of salvation. Thus the issue I want to address now is not—emphatically not—the substitution of one cultural or political agenda for another. Rather, it is the issue of placing any such agenda into the place that is reserved for the gospel in the faith and the life of the church.

Allow me to explicate this point in somewhat personal terms. My own politico-cultural positions have much to do with the insights I believe to have gained over the years of working as a social scientist. While by definition these insights have no inerrancy and are always open to revision as new empirical evidence comes up, I'm reasonably certain that I understand some things about the modern world. Thus, when I go to church or read church publications I'm irritated when I'm confronted with statements that I consider to be empirically flawed. I don't go to church in order to hear vulgarized, "pop" versions of my own field. The irritation deepens when these terrible simplifications are proclaimed to me in tones of utter certitude and moral urgency. Bad analysis obviously makes for bad policy, and here I'm not just intellectually irritated but morally offended. For example, when, in the name of the "preferential option for the poor" (a phrase with which, in principle, I have no quarrel), policies are presented as moral imperatives which, in my understanding, are likely to increase rather than reduce poverty (such as all the socialist and quasisocialist panaceas proposed for the Third World by liberation theologians—and Third World development has been my major concern for the better part of my career as a sociologist), I'm more than irritated: I'm constrained to make the moral judgment that what goes on here is profoundly irresponsible. Being human, I'm sure that I would be less irritated, and less offended, if what I heard in church were, in my understanding, more competent analysis and more responsible politics. *Nevertheless*, not for one moment am I advocating here that *my* analysis and *my* politics should be substituted for the left-of-center rhetoric rampant in our churches today (I'm speaking, of course, of the mainline Protestant and Catholic churches). *Neither* side's agenda belongs in the pulpit, in the liturgy, or in any statements that claim to have the authority of the gospel. *Any* cultural or political agenda embellished with such authority is a manifestation of "works righteousness" and ipso facto an act of apostasy.

This theological proposition, over and beyond all prudential moral judgments or political options, "hits" in all directions of the ideological spectrum; it "hits" the center as much as the left or the right. "Different gospels" lurk all across the spectrum. No value or institutional system, past or present or future, is to be identified with the gospel. The mission of the church is not to legitimate any status quo *or* any putative alteration of the status quo. The "okay world" of bourgeois America stands under judgment, in the light of the gospel, as does every other human society. Democracy or capitalism or the particular family arrangements of middle-class culture are not to be identified with the Christian life, and neither is any alternative political, economic, or cultural system. The vocation of the church is to proclaim the gospel, not to defend the American way of life, not to "build socialism," not even to "build a just society"—because, quite apart from the fact that we don't really know what this is, all our notions of justice are fallible and finally marred by sin. The "works righteousness" in all these "different gospels" lies precisely in the insinuation that, if only we do this or refrain from doing that, we will be saved, "justified." But, as Paul tells us, "by works of the law shall no one be justified."

In the face of all these "different gospels," the true gospel is *liberating.* As Paul puts it, "For freedom Christ has set us free; stand fast therefore, and do not submit again to a yoke of slavery" (Gal. 5:1). It seems to me that this liberating power of the gospel has two aspects. The first, of course, is the liberation from sin and death that is Christ's work for us. This liberation is at the heart of the gospel, indeed *is* the gospel. While it affects everyone who believes it in a very singular way, its import is cosmic, transcending all the structures of this world. What is more, this liberation is available only by faith; it cannot be proved or demonstrated except by faith. I would contend, though, that there is also, as it were, a lesser liberation brought about by the gospel—lesser only if compared with the world-shattering cataclysm of Christ's victory over sin and death— and this is the liberation from the bondage of mundaneness. This lesser liberation, unlike the first, can be perceived even short of faith; it is, if you will, an empirically available liberation. *The gospel liberates by relativizing all the realities of this world and all our projects in this world.*

We know—not by faith but by reason—that everything in this world is bound to perish. All men are mortal, and so are all the societies they create, even the most attractive ones. It is foolishness to act as if any one of our social constructions possesses ultimate importance or even reality. We can also know—such knowledge being one of the major if bitter fruits of the modern social sciences—that our projects in the world almost never yield the results we intend. Our actions regularly escape us, turn against us; all too often, they fail precisely in succeeding. This bitter truth is the common insight of allegedly successful conquerors and revolutionaries. History, which is the sum total of all human projects in this world, has no rationally discernible direction; only faith can perceive in it the unfolding of God's hidden purpose. Empirically, history is an unending repetition of cruelty and madness. The gospel liberates because it opens up to the eyes of faith a reality *beyond* history. The currently fashionable politicalization of the gospel, especially the one ironically called "liberation theology," restores us to the yoke of slavery that is imprisonment in history and imprisonment in the typically tragic web of our own projects in history.

I can already hear the muttered responses to what I have just said—accusations of "other-worldliness," more appropriate perhaps to Buddhism than to Christianity; instructions about the concrete, historical character of biblical revelation; a brief lesson on how Christians are supposed to be in the world, not escape from it. Need I say it? Believe me: *I know all these things.* I'm always amused when clerical types, who only yesterday emerged from some pietistic underworld to discover politics and sex, take it upon themselves to lecture me on worldliness. *The world is my proper vocation.* I know it fairly well. I especially know it in its modern and modernizing structures. I spend most of my days weltering in the affairs of this world. *I don't need you to tell me about worldliness!*

Of course Christian faith is "worldly" in the sense that this world is believed to be God's creation and history the arena of his redemptive actions. Of course the Christian is called upon to act in this world (or perhaps one should say, *most* Christians are so called upon; there is, I believe, the legitimate Christian vocation of the contemplative life). But the question is *how* we act in the world.

If we are liberated by faith, we act in the full knowledge of the precariousness and tragic unpredictability of all human projects. Most important, we act in this world *not* to be saved, *not* to attain some perfect purity or justice (which goals are not attainable), but to be of specific and necessarily limited service to others. Paul addresses himself to the Galatians on this issue when he insists that the freedom of the Christian is to be used as an opportunity for service, in love of one's neighbor (Gal. 5:13-14). Let me put this in terms as *worldly* as I can find: we get no moral brownie points for good intentions or noble goals. The moral measure of actions is their probable consequences for others. This is especially so in the case of political actions, because this is a category of actions with particularly unpredictable and potentially disastrous consequences. Precisely because of this, we are most likely to be effective politically (effective, that is, in being of service to our neighbors) if we ground ourselves in a realm beyond politics, thus becoming free to deal with political reality soberly and pragmatically. We cannot do this if we look on politics as the realm of redemption.

But let me return to the central point of these observations, which is that the church is constituted by the gospel. This is a community liberated in faith from all the constraining contingencies of both nature and society: "There is neither Jew nor Greek, there is neither slave nor free; there is neither male nor female" (Gal. 3:28). We know, of course, that in this world no Christian group has ever lived up to this promise, but commitment to it is an essential part of what the church purports to be. For this reason, catholicity has been counted among the "marks of the church." That catholicity is denied if a Christian community excludes people on such grounds as race, class, or gender. It seems very clear that catholicity is also denied if people are excluded on the ground of political affiliation or allegiance.

This is the final ecclesial implication of the politicalization of the church: *wherever a political agenda is seen as constitutive of the church, all those who dissent from it are excluded from the church. In that very instant, the church is no longer catholic; indeed, it ceases to be the church.*

If I am told from the pulpit, or by the language employed in the liturgy, or in public pronouncements of church authorities, that a particular political agenda is mandatory for Christians, this has ecclesial as well as moral implications. If I cannot in good conscience subscribe to this agenda, I'm implicity (perhaps, of course, even explicitly) excluded from the Christian community. To take another ironic example, if the liturgy is translated into so-called "inclusive language" (which is, in fact, an ideological jargon), then this very language excludes anyone who cannot in good conscience subscribe to the feminist agenda that the language represents. Empirically of course, this is exactly what this linguistic strategy does in our churches today. But, *mutatis mutandis*, the same exclusion occurs when *any* political or cultural agenda is elevated to the status of "gospel," no matter whether this agenda is of the right, the left, or the center. And here is the ultimate irony: *all such politicalization is an act of implicit excommunication. But, in politicizing its message, the church is in actuality excommunicating itself!*

Finally, with some reluctance, I have to make some comments about one troubling phrase in the passage that I read at the beginning of this lecture—the phrase, applied to one who preaches a "different gospel": *"let him be accursed."* (Actually, Paul uses the phrase *twice* in the passage; perhaps out of embarrassment, I've read it only once.) *"Anáthema ésto."* Such a phrase jars the ears of most of us who do not reside on the wilder shores of Protestant fundamentalism (or possibly in the secret chambers of the Roman Curia). And let me quickly reassure you that I'm not about to conclude here by hurling anathemas: I'm in the business of hypotheses, not curses. However, even if none of us are prepared to claim the apostolic *exousia* by which Paul felt authorized to utter this terrible phrase, we may usefully reflect why the preaching of "different gospels" in the church might merit a curse.

I can think of one very good reason indeed: *because this false preaching denies ministry to those who desperately need it.* Our congregations are full of individuals with a multitude of afflictions and sorrows, very few of which have anything to do with the allegedly great issues of history. These individuals come to receive the consolation and solace of the gospel, instead of which they get a lot of politics. I can think of no clearer case of one asking for bread and being given a stone. Some time ago a friend of mine went through a

very difficult period when it was suspected that he might be suffering from cancer. It turned out later that this was not the case, but
during this anxiety-ridden period neither he nor his family was
given any attention by the clergy or the active members of his congregation. This is a congregation famous for its social and political
activism. No one was interested in what, compared with the allegedly great historic challenges of our age, was the trivial matter of
one man's fear of pain and death. The people of this congregation
had more important things to do—attacking the "root causes" of
hunger by lobbying in Washington, organizing to "show solidarity"
with Nicaragua, going on record ("making a moral stand") against
apartheid. My friend says that during this time he felt like an invisible man in that congregation. Needless to say, this is a congregation that religiously employs "inclusive language." (Again, I can
hear some mutterings: Can one not lobby in Washington and *also*
minister to the sick? Perhaps. In this case, the first activity precluded
the second. And one may reflect that it is easier to love people in distant lands than people next door.)

And this case leads me to a further reflection: perhaps no apostolic anathema is required to damn the gospels of works righteousness. *The course is built-in.* Put differently, *those who put their
faith in these works in the end damn themselves.* And here again, it seems
to me that this process can be perceived empirically, even without
faith. Paul describes the unredeemed as "slaves to the elemental
spirits of the universe" (Gal. 4:3). Yes, I too have read Bultmann; I too
am a modern man, who uses electric razors and antibiotic medica-
tions, and I'm not sure (though I'm not prepared to exclude the possibility) that I believe in the sinister beings that Paul evidently had
in mind. But I do think that the processes of history and politics,
which I don't have to believe in because I know them all too well,
may safely be included among the powers to whom we are enslaved
in this world. The gospel promises us liberation from *all* these
powers, be they historical or metahistorical, natural or supernatural.
What a terrible thing it is to turn away from this promise to the vain
pseudosalvations of social existence! Here indeed is a curse, but it is
a self-activating one. Paul tells us as much: "Whatever a man sows,
that he will also reap. For he who sows to his own flesh will from the
flesh reap corruption" (Gal. 6:7-8). That corruption too is "empirically available": it is the harvest of unintended consequences, bitter
disappointments, and tormenting guilt that is reaped by those who
seek justification by political acts.

There is a form of discourse much favored by intellectuals such as myself that may be called "crisis speech." It consists of portraying an awful crisis and then suggesting that this crisis is about to happen *unless* the author's recommendations are promptly adopted. I'm tempted, but I cannot quite conform to this formula. Speaking sociologically, I don't really see any great crisis. American society is, overall, in fairly robust condition. Its class conflicts are more likely to end in compromise than in conflagration. The various religious groups will adapt or fail to adapt to change, and if some of them (especially the denominations of mainline Protestantism) end up as rather marginal sects, I, for one, would not see this as a major catastrophe. Speaking theologically, there is a crisis of ultimate seriousness—it is the crisis brought on by the gospel being proclaimed, or not proclaimed, in any moment of history—yet it is a crisis that has been with the church from its beginning.

We are justified by faith. This means that nothing depends on us. Our personal destiny and that of the entire world rests in God's hands. It also means that everything depends on us. We are called, to the best of our ability, to serve both church and world. I have said very little in this lecture about serving the world; most of my professional work is devoted to worrying about this and, when I'm active politically, to doing a few things in this department. Serving the church today, I believe, must begin with an understanding of the specific forms of apostasy that confront us today; we must recall the true meaning of gospel, church, and ministry, and then put our ecclesial houses in better order. I see very little evidence of any of this happening in American Christianity today. But then, if we believe that the Holy Spirit is active in the church, we must also believe that its actions cannot be predicted. When the Spirit revitalizes the church, it has the surprising quality of a summer thunderstorm. I wish for all of us that, in our lifetimes, we may yet be so surprised.

Secular Justifications of Christian Truth-Claims: A Historical Sketch

James Turner

I approached the assignment suggested in my title with, if not fear and trembling, at least the emotion more typical of our times, fear of confusing. I am neither theologian nor historian of theology nor even historian of religion but a historian of American intellectual life interested in the religious side of intellectual history. Writing for an audience largely composed of precisely the sorts of expert I am not, I ought first to explain my perspective. I write straightforwardly as a secular historian, hoping to contribute not a theologically grounded position but a background against which others—and perhaps myself—can proceed to argue theologically grounded positions.

What follows, then, is a brief historical sketch of how religious leaders over the past three or four centuries have justified the truth-claims of Christianity to an increasingly skeptical world.[1] Such justification has involved two distinguishable (though rarely distinct) acts: assertions of the *validity* of Christian truths and assertions of their *significance*. Anxious to secure traditional Christian beliefs against the dissolution of traditional culture, many church leaders designed these assertions to conform to emergent intellectual and social orders. The outcome, crudely put, was to subject religious truth-claims to standards of judgment structured to assess secular truths.

This blunt yet possibly delphic conclusion requires a gloss; the

---

1. In much of this essay, especially its earlier portions, I rely heavily on my book *Without God, without Creed: The Origins of Unbelief in America,* New Studies in American Intellectual and Cultural History (Baltimore: The Johns Hopkins University Press, 1985).

rest of this essay may be regarded as commentary on it. Doubtless much of the tale will be familiar, but it needs to be told of a piece in order fully to appreciate the denouement. In pursuing the story, both the example of Peter Berger's Erasmus Lecture and the direction of my own research encourage a focus on America and, within America, on Protestant leadership. But, since nothing has its roots in America (except situation comedy), one must begin in Western Europe, in the age of Reformation.

The extraordinary complexity—even downright confusion—of the cultural and social scene in early modern Europe demands of the historian prudence and discrimination. Available space permits neither; so, to begin: three important developments transformed the environment of religious thought in the sixteenth and seventeenth centuries.

First was the progress of institutional secularization, resulting from state formation, monarchical ambitions, mercantile capitalism, and the need to preserve civil peace in the wake of the religious wars set off by the Reformation. Erratically but persistently, these factors diminished the range of affairs directly under the purview of the church while increasing the range of affairs under the control of the state or secular corporations of one sort or another. Secularization did not of itself raise questions about religious truths, but it did ease the way for public debate about religious claims, making it far more common and far more probing, especially since the advent of printing had also facilitated the circulation of ideas.[2]

Specifically, by weakening churchly influence over intellectual life, secularization opened the door for arguments that earlier might have been locked out of the public domain. The medical student burned for heresy in Edinburgh in 1697 likely would have taken little comfort from the fact that he was to be the last to suffer that fate in Britain, but that simple fact goes a long way to explaining the far more radical face of public religious controversy in Britain in the

---

2. The now standard historical study of the impact of printing on early modern Europe is Elizabeth Eisenstein's *The Printing Press as an Agent of Change*, 2 vols. (Cambridge: Cambridge University Press, 1978). But attempts to understand the broad implications of "print culture" for intellectual life have been strongly influenced by the work of Walter J. Ong, S.J., beginning with his *Ramus, Method, and the Decay of Dialogue: From the Art of Discourse to the Art of Reason* (Cambridge: Harvard University Press, 1958). See especially his essays collected in *The Presence of the Word: Some Prolegomena for Cultural and Religious History* (New Haven: Yale University Press, 1967) and *Rhetoric, Romance, and Technology: Studies in the Interaction of Expression and Culture* (Ithaca: Cornell University Press, 1971).

eighteenth century as compared to the sixteenth. Yet probably more important was the not-so-simple fact that a growing proportion of thinking went on in contexts divorced from any church. Oxford remained at least a quasiecclesiastical institution, but the Royal Exchange and Royal Society did not.

Mention of the Royal Society raises the second key development: the Scientific Revolution. Copernicus, Galileo, and Newton raised no fundamental problems for Christian belief, but they did provoke awkward questions; that these issues were *not* fundamental was by no means obvious at the time. Christian truth-claims were so commonly cast in terms of old cosmologies, old physics, that the collapse of Ptolemy's and Aristotle's universes seriously unsettled understandings of Christianity. What did the contradictions between the telescope and the Bible imply about the divine authority of Scripture? What did mechanically invariant natural laws mean for providence? John Milton, likely a Copernican at heart, framed *Paradise Lost* in a medieval universe not only because it was more familiar to his readers but because it was more fitted to the doctrine of the fall. Watching that universe crumble, John Donne lamented, "'Tis all in pieces, all cohaerence gone."[3] Queen Christina of Sweden anxiously asked Descartes whether the new astronomy would subvert Christian belief.

Such intellectual difficulties became particularly urgent because religious disharmonies were increasingly scored in an intellectual key. In medieval Europe, and indeed among the first generation of Reformers, "belief" carried far more the sense of "belief in" (a person, in the sense of confidence, reliance) than "belief that" (such-and-such a proposition is true)—just as "religion" meant dominantly something like "religious practice" or "piety." Doctrine, significant though it was, took very distinctly a back seat to communal ritual or personal devotion in the conception of what Christianity meant. By the late sixteenth century, if not earlier, the meanings of "belief" had begun to gravitate toward their modern balance of connotations. "Belief" never lost the sense of "trust," but its propositional or intellectual meaning loomed larger.

Ironically, the Reformers, intending to exalt the role of faith in salvation, unintentionally also magnified the intellectual dimension of Christianity. As the Reformation fragmented in a clash of doctrines after 1517, exfoliation of creeds provided the distinguish-

---

3. John Donne, "The First Anniversarie," in *The Complete Poetry of John Donne*, ed. John T. Shawcross (New York: New York University Press, 1967), pp. 270, 277-78.

ing marks of different Protestantisms, and leaders of the Roman
Church (old hands at the business of creed-making) proved, at Trent
and later, at least a match for their competition. Indeed, theological
warfare during the sixteenth and seventeenth centuries fostered an
obsession with doctrinal distinctions drawn so fine as almost to dis-
appear before a modern eye. Although *Pietismus* in Germany and
similar reactions elsewhere eventually restrained some of this enthusiasm for slivering dogma, Christians continued to *define* themselves—as Lutherans, Catholics, Presbyterians, whatever—largely
on the basis of rather precisely formulated intellectual disagreements.

Thus, when church leaders tried to reformulate and defend
Christian truths in the volatile intellectual climate and ungov-
ernable public arena of early modern Europe, they were tempted to
see their problem as largely intellectual. And it is important to understand that their construction of the situation, though originating
in early modern Europe, outlasted the seventeenth century to
remain the characteristic structuring of this sort of apologetic up to
our own time. As the effects of secularization and the influence of
science penetrated ever more deeply into cultural realms once
dominated by the church, church leaders of the nineteenth and
twentieth centuries continued to understand their task in confront-
ing "modernity" as quintessentially coming to *intellectual* terms
with it.

To take one fairly extreme but well-known instance, modern creationists defend their (propositional) version of Christian truth by
producing a nonstandard version of biology. They insist it is not
Christian biology but simply biology, and therefore refutable by
biological research—thereby setting biological science in judgment
over Christian truth. At the other end of the spectrum of accom-
modation to evolutionism, Pierre Teilhard de Chardin's theological
writings exhibit an impulse similar in principle. By molding Christian revelation to what he supposed were the revelations of paleon-
tology, Teilhard left Christian truth-claims exposed to scientific cor-
rosion. What happens to the Omega Point if biologists decide that
devolution is the ultimate fate of life? To be sure, Teilhard's project,
explicitly speculative, was to that extent less risky than that of the
creationists.

To seventeenth-century Christian apologists, the contemporary
cultural landscape often looked as bleak and frightening as it sometimes does to twentieth-century fundamentalists. Christian truth—
in fact, belief in God—seemed fragile and endangered. The depth of
this anxiety explains the otherwise puzzling, unquestionably

widespread fear of atheism at a time when, to say the least, atheism was severely shorthanded. And one can sympathize with their worries. Whatever Paul Tillich's theological merits, he was surely right to insist that symbols adequate to express faith in one cultural context may prove woefully inadequate in another. With traditional conceptions of providence, hell, and biblical truth falling into ruins along with the medieval worldviews that had supported them— while members of the once catholic church debated doctrine by cutting each other's throats—some adjustments seemed prudent.

Reinterpreting and defending Christian truth-claims was far from the leading concern of most church leaders; salvaging their own flocks and savaging other Christians easily outranked the broad apologetic task. But for our purposes, understanding the apologetic strategies adopted is crucial. There were essentially two. One was to ground religious belief intellectually in the very structure of knowledge that seemed most immediately to threaten it: the methods and data of natural science. The most spectacularly successful example of this approach was the argument from design, pioneered in natural history by John Ray, elaborated in cosmology and astronomy by Samuel Clarke (under the tutelage of the great Newton himself), and codified at the end of the eighteenth century by William Paley, whose *Natural Theology* exercised generations of college students until one of them, Charles Darwin, used the evidences of design to subvert the Designer. The argument from design did not prove a specifically Christian God, but it seemed to prove a God; and, with that premise established, apologists could extend their chain of logic and evidence to the validity of the Christian revelation.

The other strategic ploy was to stress the down-to-earth moral benefits of Christianity at the expense of its less easily graspable truth-claims. This emphasis had multiple advantages. First, it played down apparently unreasonable and mysterious elements of Christianity (such as the Trinity), and hence made Christianity seem more rational, or at least less irrational, when viewed against the background of modern science. Second, moralism offered a platform for Christian unity, since all Christians could presumably agree on the moral lessons of their religion; apologists thus hoped to put aside the scandal of a century of religious bloodshed and strife and make Christianity appear a force for peace in a quarrelsome world. Third, painting Christianity as primarily aimed at moral improve-ment aligned the church with the progressive forces of science, commerce, technology, and enlightenment. When the fashionable Congregationalist preacher Jonathan Mayhew in the mid-eighteenth century described Christianity to his Boston congregation as "principally an institution of life and manners, designed to teach us how to be good men," he was not speaking to the *validity* of Christian truth-claims but stressing their *significance* for building a durable, humane, and civilized society.[4] Yet such assertions of Christianity's moral import were, every bit as much as scientific demonstrations of its truth, intended to secure the authority of Christianity.

Both types of assertion had the consequence (sometimes unintended) of thrusting into the background the otherworldly, transcendental, ungraspable character of much religious experience—the ultimate "otherness" of the divine. Both types of assertion advanced Christian truth-claims in the same epistemological and moral arenas as the now largely secular truths of science and politics. And both types of assertion proved remarkably successful.

There is no denying that Christianity had a rocky time in elite circles during the eighteenth century. (Reliable general assessments of its fate among less favored folk are only just beginning to be pieced together by historians in both Europe and America. Initial impressions suggest an upswing rather than the reverse.) Certainly —to narrow our aperture now to America—Christianity faced an uphill struggle among the seaboard elites of the newly independent United States. By 1790 Deists may have outnumbered orthodox Christians among the wealthy planters of Virginia and South Carolina, and a lot of Boston Unitarians shared Deist beliefs if not the label. Yet, in longer historical perspective, Deism and other forms of Enlightenment natural religion appear nothing more than an extreme version of the effort to modernize Christianity: Franklin and Jefferson now look not like pagans but like Christians who have stripped their religion of mystery, brought it intellectually in line with science, and turned it primarily toward moral improvement. It comes as no surprise then that Deism faded back into Christianity as rapidly as it had emerged from it.

What erased Deism was the force that created American Protestantism as we now know it: the great evangelical revivals of the early nineteenth century—the so-called Second Great Awakening.[5] Evangelicalism triumphed with astonishing speed. In 1790 Deist ideas had ornamented the best parlors of Massachusetts and Virginia; by 1830 they belonged only to aging relics and shrill outcasts.

---

4. Jonathan Mayhew, *Seven Sermons* (Boston, 1749).
5. Astonishingly, we still lack a full-length general study of the Second Great Awakening, though it was arguably the most important single event (if it is reasonable to call it a "single event") in American cultural history.

Yet, while evangelicals restored to primacy traditional Christian doctrines and a gracious relationship with a personal Savior, they also continued with remarkable fidelity the moralizing and intellectualizing strategies of their Enlightenment ancestors. They continued to preach a God demonstrable by (though certainly not saving through) modern science, a faith defined (though by no means entirely defined) in terms of logical propositions, a Christianity oriented toward (though not limited to) the moral improvement of human society.

Yet to call the evangelical enterprise secular would be patently absurd. These devout and energetic men and women drew no such distinction between God's work and the world's. They believed in scientific truth as fervently as biblical truth because they knew that both were God's truth and each supported the other. They believed that the church's mission in this world included improving the conditions of human life as well as saving souls because they knew that God intended to work with human hands, human science, and human legislation to make this world fit to be his kingdom. Far from suspecting science or social change of being threats to Christian truth, they embraced both as manifestations of God's providence— a providence often achieving its moral ends through the natural laws revealed by science.

The long campaign, begun in the seventeenth century, to secure Christian truth by accommodating it to modern realities had, at least in America, fulfilled the dreams of its progenitors. The historian, accustomed to the swift wreckage of human schemes, can only marvel at its extraordinary success. America probably came closer to being a "Christian nation" (in a Protestant version) in the mid-nineteenth century than ever before or since, and its Christianity was founded squarely on the divinization of modern science and social reform. What perhaps most surprises our jaded eyes is the effervescent self-confidence of evangelical leaders, its quintessential manifestation being the optimistic millennialism that was common currency among mainstream Protestants in the antebellum decades. The (post)millennialism of such great evangelical theologians and activists as Samuel Hopkins and Lyman Beecher differed sharply from the pessimistic premillennialism of many of today's fundamentalists.[6] Where the latter functions to set religious faith against

___

6. Reading the rather eccentric, if not bizarre, *Autobiography* (1864) of Lyman Beecher remains perhaps the best entry into the world of the Second Great Awakening. (There is a modern version edited by Barbara M. Cross published in two volumes [Cambridge: Harvard University Press, 1961].) Samuel Hopkins's *Treatise on the Millennium* (Boston,

secular hopes, the former tended to merge Christianity and the world. The millennium was to be hurried on by science, technology, education, and melioristic legislation as much as by preaching and praying. Indeed, the millennial visions of Protestant leaders in this period are often hard to distinguish from the utopias dreamed slightly later by prophets of science and technology such as Edward Bellamy. The lasting legacy of this confidence in the reigning culture was the *Kulturprotestantismus* to which Peter Berger refers.

Whether or not pride goeth before a fall, confidence generally does. Although *Kulturprotestantismus* endured, the triumphant wedding of Christianity and science ended in divorce before the century was two-thirds gone. As is often the case, the contesting parties anxiously tried to patch up the relationship, denied that anything fundamental had gone wrong, exchanged angry recriminations, and finally went their separate ways. The depressing details need not be retold here. Darwinism provided probably the most important bone of contention, but biblical criticism, anthropology, and the study of comparative religion all played into the quarreling.[7] What happened was not that scientists turned against Christianity. (The hoary metaphor of warfare between Science and Religion ought to have been buried long ago; most American scientists probably remained churchgoing Christians into the early twentieth century.) Rather, as the epistemological and metaphysical focus of science sharpened and became exclusively centered on the physical world, and as scientists denied any wider reach of scientific conclusions, reference to science for evidence of God became increasingly implausible. One might say that Darwin touched off the final burst of secularization in the intellectual realm.

Part of the fallout from this explosion was the emergence of agnosticism as an intellectually viable option; but I have told that story elsewhere, and it is in any case peripheral to my argument here. More relevant was the reaction of clergy, theologians, and other intellectuals concerned—concerned both pastorally and personally—to maintain solid foundations for belief. Most Christians, it should

---

1793) provides a quite typical picture of the imagined millennium and shows how even a sober, first-rate theologian shared the vision of a religiotechnological utopia.

7. The University of Wisconsin Press will soon publish Jon Roberts's study of American Protestant responses to "Darwinism" (if I may use that term, not quite precisely, to mean theories of organic evolution) between 1859 and 1900, which will be the most thorough and reliable assessment of the question.

be said, probably went their way undisturbed by, or even unaware of, these problems: the usual indicators suggest that American churches flourished in the late nineteenth century. But the usual indicators indicated little about the feelings—often approaching panic—of Christians who took their religion with *intellectual* seriousness.

There was, most immediately, a good deal of scrambling to find something other than physical science out of which to cobble together bases for religious truth-claims. Much of late-nineteenth-century American philosophy was motivated by this sometimes desperate sense of uncertainty. Consider Royce's idealism and James's pragmatism (and, more obvious though less strictly philosophical, his *Varieties of Religious Experience*). A similar anxious adaptation appeared very quickly in American theology. Contrast, for example, the self-assured laying out of "obvious" "proofs" of the existence of God as late as 1855 in the fourth edition of James McCosh's *Method of Divine Government* with the chastened, tentative (but also far subtler and more complex) effort by George T. Ladd in *Bibliotheca Sacra* in 1877 to suggest some intellectually plausible groundings for faith in God.[8]

Whatever one's judgment about the success of these attempts, it is quite clear that Christian apologists—and, for that matter, non-Christian theists—felt themselves on the defensive intellectually. And they were right; they *were* on the defensive intellectually. This was precisely the position that they had readied for themselves from the seventeenth century when they attached belief to a science busy focusing itself on physical nature. In fairness, their strategy as originally devised was far from contemptible. It expressed their faith in the power of Christianity to comprehend the world; it manifested their conviction that any faith worth keeping had to bring its adherents into living relation with the currents of their age; and, for a very long time, it worked spectacularly well.

Yet the insistence of Christian apologists on the scientific rationality of Christianity entailed also a neglect of the mysterious and transcendent, a neglect of their religion's maxim that, although Christianity might comprehend the world, the world could not define Christianity nor comprehend God. To secure Christianity in down-to-earth realities, they set aside their sense of transcendent

---

8. James McCosh, *The Method of the Divine Government, Physical and Moral*, 4th ed. (New York, 1855); George T. Ladd, "The Difficulties of the Concept of God," *Bibliotheca Sacra*, 34 (1877): 631 et passim.

realities, their sense of the complexity of wending one's way through both their world and their God's world, their sense of balance. To hold to Christian faith is, I should judge, intellectually much less disreputable today than in the late nineteenth century. But, vis-à-vis the dominant forms of knowledge in our culture, Christian truth-claims are still on the defensive. And it is important for us to understand that, historically, Christian leaders played a large role in putting them there.

Despite rapid theological reconstruction, then, assertions of the *validity* of Christian truth-claims continued to appear dubious, especially when set next to the truth-claims of science. The second-rate character of its truths put religion at a great disadvantage in an era committed to an essentially positivistic approach to knowledge, as the late nineteenth and early twentieth centuries were. Most Americans never lost their Christian faith, but intellectually alert Americans (including ministers) often found their beliefs harder to justify, found themselves troubled by qualms of doubt.

In these circumstances, it appeared critically important to many religious leaders to underscore the *significance* of Christian truths. Stressing the social importance—as distinguished from reliability— of Christian truth-claims was anything but a Machiavellian ploy by preachers to rescue their foundering churches. They had been preaching for a century, after all, that the future of the Republic lay in Protestantism, indeed that the trajectory of the Protestant Republic ended in the millennium. They deeply believed that the world was redeemable and that God had charged their churches with the mission to redeem it through social and ethical reform. Yet they realized as well that this social emphasis could push aside troubling questions about the epistemological validity of Christian beliefs. At a time when belief in transcendent realities often seemed shaky if not disreputable, turning attention to the urgent needs of this earth gave the churches a breather. Moral conviction fitted nicely with intellectual expediency.

However, down this road, too, lay perils. Reform-minded church leaders cast their appeal, quite naturally, along the roads mapped out by the great evangelical social reformers of preceding generations. The gospel message, they said, required the ethical and physical transformation first of American society and then of less-favored regions. Like Samuel Hopkins and Lyman Beecher, this younger generation believed that science and technology, education and legislation, would provide the tools for building the kingdom of God (though in the Social Gospel of the late nineteenth and early twentieth centuries "science" commonly meant reformist social science).[9] But whereas Hopkins and Beecher still stressed the salvation of the individual and generally located sin very personally in the irresponsible drunkard or callous slaveholder, Social Gospelers such as Washington Gladden and Walter Rauschenbusch spoke of the salvation of society and pointed the finger of guilt at the wealthy and powerful, suggesting that they were responsible for such social sins as alcoholism and racism. Indeed, *sin*, a word laden with unfortunate connotations of that misty otherworld, tended to fade into vaguer notions of social evils, less off-putting to the secular-minded.

This studied blurring of the boundaries between secular and transcendent did not mean that a Social Gospel outfit like the Federal (later National) Council of Churches became essentially nonreligious. Precisely the contrary: the whole point was to ensure that secular reform *remained* religious, remained linked to the gospel and the churches. Otherwise, Social Gospelers commonly believed, assertions of the significance of Christianity would fall flat. This outlook makes clearer why a Rauschenbusch, however sympathetic with the work of nonreligious reformers, insisted on the *independent* leadership role of the church.

Nevertheless, committing churches to social reform did effectually link Christianity—in its Social Gospel version—to the progressive vision of limitless social improvement through technical innovation. Peter Berger's discussion of the "New Class" points to the social side of this cultural phenomenon. (I would, however, locate the bifurcation of the middle class earlier historically than he, though agreeing on the enormous expansion of the "New Class" in post–World War II America.) The social scientists, the professional "educators," the social workers—the social experts of all stripes—represented precisely that ethos, originally sited more specifically in natural science, where intellectual and moral authority had come to center. It was to this authority that many religious leaders were trying to hitch their wagons. As post-Newtonian natural theologians had tied the *validity* of Christian truth-claims to physical science, so Social Gospelers at the turn of the century linked the *significance* of Christian truth-claims to social science, broadly defined. And even Reinhold Niebuhr's momentous attack on the Social Gospel in the 1930s struck not at its neglect of transcendence but at its failure to be worldly enough.

---

9. American intellectual historians are still trying to assess the obviously central but nevertheless elusive moral role of science in late nineteenth- and early twentieth-century American culture. David A. Hollinger's forthcoming book on the subject should go a long way toward helping us get a better grasp of this problem.

Where would this lead? The hoped-for outcome was the sanctification of secular reform. (Though this was decidedly not the only result intended. It would be grossly unfair to denigrate the Social Gospelers' sincere conviction of the church's duty to reform the world.) Another possible outcome was the secularization of religious reform—that is, a drift out of the churches of those individuals who accepted the reform message of the Social Gospel but felt no need for the often thin penumbra of Christian doctrine around it. If the moral renovation of American society was the essential religious task and if this task was best accomplished by political action and social-scientific expertise, then why were churches and Christianity necessary? In short, the truth-claims of Christianity might face a crisis of *insignificance* comparable to the nineteenth-century crisis of *invalidity*.

The jury, it must be said, is still out. Certainly no historian—a notoriously pusillanimous breed at best—would dare to claim that the outcome is clear. On the one hand, Peter Berger is probably right in pointing out that the current drift away from the mainstream Protestant churches results in part from dissatisfaction with their Social-Gospelish agenda. On the other hand, we do not know enough about the reasons for or directions of the drift. We do not know, for example, whether the unchurched have unchurched themselves because they reject the mainstream churches' social vision or because they think that they can achieve it more effectively without the churches. We do not know whether the new evangelicals mostly hunger for transcendence or for a right-wing version of the Social Gospel.

In my analysis (as in Berger's), the Moral Majority is not in a radically different position from the National Council of Churches. The roots of the Social Gospel, I have argued, trace back to the religiosocial reform project of pre–Civil War evangelicals. The Moral Majority shares this pedigree, though it remains much closer to the moralistic outlook of antebellum evangelicalism—stripped, to be sure, of its postmillennial theological foundation. (Again one sees the cultural side of Berger's class analysis: the "old bourgeoisie" maintaining the Victorian culture in which it achieved its most flourishing growth.) One should not exaggerate the cousinship of left- and right-wing American social Protestantism: Jerry Falwell could hardly be described as preaching jihad in behalf of social science and technical expertise. But, *to the extent* that the Moral Majority gives primacy to promoting social change, including renovation of values and mores, its agenda is also, though probably not so easily, liable to secularization. A return to "traditional

values" can well be promoted under the label of—dare I say it?—
humanism.

Moving beyond Protestantism, the picture is equally obscure.
The recent record of American Catholicism provides as good a
reason to argue that a social-reform agenda deepens religious commitment as to argue the reverse. The experience of Reform Judaism
over the past century would seem to suggest that social religion
promotes secularization. But then what are we to make of the
tangled history of Zionism in this respect? And so it goes.

But now I am slipping beyond the self-imposed limits of the
historian's role. Having done so, let me ask what any layperson (and
few historians) would ask: Are there any immediate practical lessons to be drawn from this story? At the risk of demonstrating my
own inutility, I confess to being dubious. There is surely an inevitable tension between the Christian orientation to transcendence
and the equally Christian imperative to serve others, which must include making religious beliefs meaningful in this world's terms—
whatever that may mean. One can safely say that Protestant leaders
since the Reformation have often neglected the requisite balance in
their zeal to shore up belief. Committing Christian truth-claims to
essentially scientific standards of truth had disastrous results, and
my own guess is that any heavily politicized version of Christianity
will receive the same punishment. Yet to have refused to face up to
the intellectual challenge of modern science would likely have
relegated Christianity to the cultural attic where quaint antique ar-
tifacts are stored. And to pull back from social challenges such as
nuclear war and mass misery might have similar consequences.

Historical analysis provides no basis for easy distinctions between the transcendent and salvific mission of the church on the one
hand and surrender to some worldly agenda (intellectual or social)
on the other. Peter Berger refers to the problem of traditional versus
"inclusive" language in the liturgy. He argues that the adoption of
"nonsexist" language has the effect of excluding many tradition-
minded members of a congregation, and he is right. But he ignores
the awkward fact that continuing use of traditional language has the
effect of excluding many feminist-minded members, though likely
fewer, at least in most American churches at present. Does one
choose whom to exclude? On the basis of numbers? Does one try to
improvise some sort of via media that will enable the church to minister to as many as possible? (And the devil take the thoroughgoing
ideologues on both sides?) Does one accept a pluralism of ministries
and liturgies?

I see no clear answer—to this or the many analogous conundrums. And I doubt that Peter Berger's formula—the primacy of the gospel as against contingent and fallible social and political agenda—gives a straightforward answer either. Contemporary Christians can learn from the errors and excesses of religious leaders of the past, as from their wisdom and successes, but they cannot escape their dilemmas. To be sure, if Christianity is to remain Christian, then Christians must never forget the primacy of the gospel: that is, in my view, the central moral of the history I have related. But if the message of the gospel is unchanging, its expression cannot be; if the cross and resurrection are given us as eternal truths, their meanings remain to be explored by human beings in temporality.

And that is surely another moral of this historical sketch. What the primacy of the gospel *means* and how it is to be proclaimed have in the past necessarily been worked out on the ground, in the flux of historically local, contingent, and temporary circumstance, with much variation from place to place and time to time. More bluntly, (1) the apostasy that Berger describes has (as he suggests) likely been as prevalent at other times as now, and (2) what counts as works-righteousness has (as he does not make clear) rarely been transparent at any time, however obvious it may seem in the long view—that last phrase meaning, of course, "however it looks to us from our local point in time."

I suspect that groping and confusion will continue to be the human condition, religiously as otherwise. It seems apt to conclude as Berger began, with a nonsermonic invocation of St. Paul. Here, however, the application of St. Paul's message is, appropriately, less certain: "Be not forgetful to entertain strangers: for thereby some have entertained angels unawares" (Heb. 13:2, KJV).

Gospel, Church, and Politics

Avery Dulles, S.J.

In my invitation to participate in this conference, I was asked to present a constructive Catholic position and to use my own discretion in deciding whether to respond directly to Peter Berger's Erasmus Lecture. In the major portion of this paper I intend to develop what I understand to be an acceptable Roman Catholic approach to the conference theme. Then in a concluding section I shall compare my own position with that of Berger, as gleaned from the early draft of his lecture that was available to me. My constructive section will deal successively with the gospel, the church, and the magisterium, each considered in relation to the sociopolitical order. I shall trace the role of the magisterium prior to Vatican Council II, at the Council, and since the Council, with close attention to the pastoral letters of the United States Episcopal Conference, *The Challenge of Peace* (1983) and *Economic Justice for All* (1986). In my personal reflections I shall attempt to show the legitimacy of the church's concern for social order while at the same time cautioning against the politiciza-

---

NOTE: The following abbreviations are used in this essay:

AA   *Apostolicam actuositatem:* The Decree on the Apostolate of the Laity

CP   *The Challenge of Peace*

DH   *Dignitatis humanae:* The Declaration on Religious Liberty

EJ   *Economic Justice for All*

GS   *Gaudium et spes:* The Pastoral Constitution on the Church in the Modern World

JW   *Justice in the World*

LG   *Lumen gentium:* The Dogmatic Constitution on the Church

OA   *Octogesima adveniens:* A Call to Action

PO   *Presbyterorum ordinis:* The Decree on the Life and Ministry of Priests

SC   *Sacrosanctum concilium:* The Constitution on the Sacred Liturgy

tion of religion. My positions will be in line with what I understand to have been the major thrust of the Hartford Appeal of 1975—namely, that by regaining its sense of transcendence the church can best overcome the threat to its own relevance.

THE GOSPEL AND GOD'S NEW ORDER

To those who are inclined—as most of us are—to fashion the divinity in the likeness of the human, Jesus responds by proposing a vastly different idea of God. The God of the Gospels, *pace* Feuerbach, is not a projection of human ideals, nor is divine justice simply human justice writ large. While the God of Jesus is in some respects like a good human father or ruler, he frequently behaves in ways that would be unacceptable in human affairs. In the world disclosed by Jesus, divine approval is given to the dishonest manager who craftily remits the debts owed to his master. In another parable God is likened to an employer who rewards laborers who have worked for a single hour with the same wages as those who have borne the heat of an entire day. Yet again, God is compared to an unjust judge who reluctantly gives in to the demands of petitioners who annoy him by their persistence. God enriches those who are already wealthy and takes away from the poor the little that they have. He severely judges those who scrupulously fulfill their religious duties and liberally forgives tax collectors and prostitutes for the mere asking. He is ready to neglect the many righteous in order to bring back a single individual who has gone astray. God is like a miserly woman who scrapes the floor searching for a lost penny. Throughout the Gospels Jesus seems to be going out of his way to shock those who have constructed their concept of God according to human norms of dignity, virtue, and prudence. God's thoughts are not our thoughts, nor are his ways our ways.

The gospel accordingly presents us with a totally new order of things, quite unlike anything we would suspect from our experience on earth. There is a divine or transcendent order in which certain things are possible and proper that are neither possible nor fitting in worldly affairs. Jesus opens up to his hearers this higher world, asking them to accept it in faith. By his preaching he makes it possible for people to understand reality in a wholly new light. In the world people aspire to health, power, pleasure, family, friends, money, rank, and reputation. All these things are valuable here below, but Jesus teaches that they are of no value for eternity. The only thing of true and lasting importance is our standing in relation to the God whom Jesus makes known. What counts before him is purity of heart, humility, mercy. Even virtues such as honesty, thrift, learning, and industry are not enough. Trusting God, we should make no provision for the morrow. We should have no fear of those who can do nothing worse than kill the body. We should not labor for the food that perishes but only for the bread of eternal life. Not to be rich in the sight of God is the only real tragedy.

Jesus underscores this radical teaching with many sayings and parables that predict a dramatic reversal in the kingdom of God. The first will be last and the last first. The rich will become poor and the poor rich. Those content to be as slaves will be the true masters. Already, by a kind of prolepsis, infants spout wisdom, the blind see, the lame walk. "What is exalted before men is an abomination in the sight of God" (Luke 16:15). All these paradoxes and antitheses are credible only to those who believe; they are visible only to the eye of faith.

Christian dualism bears a certain analogy with Platonism. For Plato the realm of appearances was superficial and unimportant. What counted was the inward reality, known by intelligence. Whoever was truly wise would rather be just and suffer for it than be unjust and escape suffering, for virtue was of greater worth than any external benefits or rewards. For Jesus, likewise, the transitory realm of sense-appearance was unimportant. But for him the "really real" was the realm known by faith—the gift whereby one participates in God's own knowledge. True life is bestowed by Jesus and is eternal.

Paul was able to sum up this new perspective by equating the visible with the transitory and the invisible with the eternal. "We look not to the things that are seen but to the things that are unseen; for the things that are seen are transient, but the things that are unseen are eternal" (2 Cor. 4:18). The things that meant most to Paul before his conversion appear to him in Christ to be no more than rubbish (Phil. 3:8). The wisdom of this world is foolishness in the sight of God (1 Cor. 1:18-31).

It is in terms of these stark contrasts that Jesus draws up his concept of discipleship. He calls on his followers to live according to the vision of reality disclosed by faith and thus to seek the very opposite of what the world holds dear. They must be prepared to be poor rather than rich and in this way to accumulate treasure in heaven. They must be prepared to suffer in order to be blessed and to lose their life in this world in order to save it for eternity.

The community of disciples, as Jesus seems to have viewed it, was a contrast society, into which one entered not by gradual improvement but by a totally new beginning, described as rebirth. The community of the disciples, which was a kind of prelude to the Christian church, had the task of attesting through word and deed the new order disclosed by Jesus. Its first and indispensable task was to evangelize—to proclaim the way of salvation opened up by the only-begotten Son. The church became—and at its best must always remain—what Peter Berger calls a "cognitive minority," a faithful remnant of those who forsake worldly benefits in order to follow the crucified and risen Master.

In contrast to Platonism, Christianity proclaims an order that is not timeless. Eternal life has a beginning in time, even though, in principle, it has no end. And the kingdom of God exists not simply in some supercelestial realm but as a real promise for the future of this earth. With the resurrection of Jesus, the glorious transformation of creation has already begun. The church heralds and anticipates the completion of that which has been inaugurated; it certifies that the kingdom will in fact be realized. Christians are those who in faith already belong to the ultimate future that now lies hidden in God.

PROCLAIMING THE GOSPEL: FAITH AND WORKS

Although Jesus called for radical transformation, many of his followers remained to a great extent untransformed. Ever since its beginnings the church has been a *corpus mixtum* (Augustine), a net filled with good fish and bad, a field sown with good grain and darnel. The separation of the good from the evil will not occur until the parousia. In the meantime we must not try to uproot the weeds lest in doing so we damage the wheat. The church, while counting sinners in its midst, strives incessantly to purify itself.

Christians are constantly faced with the problem of how to relate the two realms in which they live. By faith they belong to the coming eschatological kingdom, but by experience they are involved in the transitory kingdom of this world. They have involvements with other human beings that do not allow them, except in rare instances, to live consistently by the precepts of the Sermon on the Mount. Lest they be found incapable of completing the tower once begun (Luke 14:28-30), they have to exercise worldly prudence. They must frequently take thought for the morrow, have recourse to law courts, defend their property rights, seek police protection, and sometimes employ military might. They cannot regularly give up their possessions to those who want to rob them nor always turn the other cheek to their assailants.

The primary task of the church is to preserve intact the message of the gospel, in all its novelty and strength. Neither the sinfulness of Christians nor the exigencies of worldly living can exempt the church from this lofty mission. While preaching the gospel by word, the church must seek to embody it in symbolic actions, notably the sacraments. But the church cannot pretend to bring about the final kingdom, which God will accomplish when and as he chooses. The promise of the kingdom rests on God's Word, which is absolutely reliable, and not on human efforts, which are forever bound by limited possibilities. Although the efforts of human beings, sustained by the grace of God, are by no means useless, such efforts could never bring about the consummation of the kingdom. The church, therefore, must urge its members to put their trust in the power and goodness of God rather than in any created agency, including even the church. God alone can save.

Granted the primacy of evangelization, it must be asked whether the church has any further responsibilities beyond holding aloft the transcendent vision proposed by Jesus and confirmed by his resurrection from the dead. I would maintain that the church has a second responsibility, from which it can by no means exempt itself. This is to guide its members, and all who wish to submit to its influence, in behaving according to the gospel. Jesus is very insistent that it is not sufficient to say "Lord, Lord," but that one must put his precepts into practice.

Jesus is strict in his interpretation of the commandments. To relax even the least of them is to make oneself least in the kingdom of God. The practices of fasting and almsgiving are praised; adultery and divorce are roundly condemned. Those who do the will of the Father count as Jesus' brothers and sisters. The evildoer will be cast into the outer darkness and will suffer the torments of eternal flames. Those who beat their fellow servants and make harsh demands on their own debtors will themselves be beaten and severely judged. Most especially will the Son of Man condemn those who close their hearts to the needs of the hungry, the naked, the sick, and the imprisoned.

FAITH AND WORKS

The early church was faithful to this aspect of the message of Jesus. Paul, for all his insistence on justification by faith, fully accepted the axiom, rooted in the Wisdom literature of the Old Testament and reechoed in Matthew, that all will be individually rewarded or punished according to their deeds in the flesh (1 Cor. 3:8; 2 Cor. 5:10). Jews as well as Greeks will receive due retribution for their works (Rom. 2:6). Admission to the kingdom will be denied to the envious, murderous, and sexually impure (Rom. 1:30). In another list Paul excludes adulterers, homosexuals, thieves, robbers, and drunkards (1 Cor. 6:9-10). In a third catalogue, he enumerates impurity, idolatry, enmity, strife, jealousy, anger, drunkenness, and the like as "works of the flesh" that exclude one from inheriting the kingdom of God (Gal. 5:19-21).

To hold that people are saved by faith alone regardless of their conduct would be a serious deformation of Paul's actual teaching. Rejecting this pseudo-Pauline position, the letter of James insists that faith without works is dead. Faith justifies only if it becomes active through works. John in his first letter calls attention to the deceptiveness of thinking that it is possible to love God without obeying the commandments. The fourth Gospel likewise teaches that those who have done good deeds will experience the "resurrection of life, and those who have done evil, the resurrection of judgment" (John 5:29).

It would be superfluous to cite these well-known texts except that it is occasionally asserted that since the church's task is to proclaim the gospel, good works are of little importance. The assumption behind this view is apparently that we are saved by faith alone and not by observing the commandments. A church that insisted on faith alone as a substitute for right conduct would not be proclaiming the gospel of Christ but, if I may say so, "another gospel" (cf. Gal. 1:6).

I am not trying here to make a polemical point for Catholics against Lutherans. In the eloquent first chapter of *The Cost of Discipleship*, Dietrich Bonhoeffer adroitly defends Luther against the charge of having proclaimed cheap grace, but he does insist, in opposition to some later Lutherans, that "costly grace is the only pure grace, which really forgives sins and gives freedom to the sinner."[1] The only person who has the right to say that he is justified by grace alone, says Bonhoeffer, is the one who has left all to follow Christ. "Those who try to use this grace as a dispensation from following Christ are simply deceiving themselves."[2]

SOCIAL ETHICS OF THE NEW TESTAMENT

For the true Christian, I take it, the question is not whether obedience and good works are needed, but which works are com-

---

1. Bonhoeffer, *The Cost of Discipleship*, 2d ed., trans. R. H. Fuller, rev. Irmgard Booth (New York: Macmillan, 1963), p. 57.
2. Bonhoeffer, *The Cost of Discipleship*, p. 55.

manded and are truly good. The New Testament, as I have indicated, gives many lists of virtues and vices, fruits of the Spirit and fruits of the flesh. These lists remain pertinent and helpful for our own day, when anger, lust, impatience, and the like pursue their destructive course in the world.

It is often said that the New Testament ethic is individualistic. In a certain sense this is true, insofar as the subject of moral behavior is generally regarded as the individual. The commendation or condemnation of nations and races as such is rather rare in the New Testament as compared with the Old. But the New Testament has a social dimension insofar as it accents virtues and vices that affect human interrelationships. In answering the question "What must I do to inherit eternal life?" Jesus goes immediately to the second table of the law: "Do not kill, do not commit adultery, do not steal, do not bear false witness, do not defraud, honor your father and mother" (Mark 10:19). Paul in Romans gives a similar list of precepts and then adds that all the commandments are summed up in the sentence, "You shall love your neighbor as yourself." Love, therefore, is the fulfillment of the law (Rom. 13:8-10; cf. Gal. 5:13).

Love, as Paul understands it, is not simply a one-on-one relationship. He sees in Christ the inauguration of a new community transcending all divisions of race, sex, nationality, and social status. "Here there cannot be Greek and Jew, circumcised and uncircumcised, barbarian, Scythian, slave, free man, but Christ is all, and in all" (Col. 3:11). Reconciled to God in Christ, the disciples are reconciled to one another and are sent into the world as agents of Christ's reconciling work. "Disunity, conflicts, and quarrels among believers," says John Coleman, "are a scandal to the unity of the one body of Christ."[3]

The ethical code of the New Testament is primarily drawn from that of ancient Judaism, especially the Decalogue. But in several respects Jesus is more radical. He is intransigent in insisting on monogamous, indissoluble marriage and in disapproving sexual intercourse outside of marriage. One also finds in the message of Jesus, especially as set forth in Luke, a bias in favor of—or, as it might be called today, a preferential option for—the poor. This is perhaps based on the fact that the poor proved more ready than the rich to accept the good news of the kingdom. However that may be, the poor are considered to be blessed, and riches are regularly portrayed as a danger to salvation. In this respect James speaks even

---

3. Coleman, *An American Strategic Theory* (New York: Paulist Press, 1982), p. 16.

more sharply than Jesus in the Gospels. The rich are told to weep and wail over their impending misfortunes. The cries of the poor, whose wages have been withheld, and those of the defrauded harvesters, have reached the ears of God (James 5:1-6).

Reading these words today, we might imagine that Jesus and the first Christians were social reformers, but of this tendency there is no trace. Jesus does nothing to arouse the poor to struggle against oppression, nor does he instruct his disciples to work for a new social order. As Ernst Troeltsch saw very clearly, "The message of Jesus is not a programme of social reform. It is rather a summons to prepare for the coming of the Kingdom of God."[4] The followers of Jesus must live in such a way that their conduct arouses hope in the imminent coming of the kingdom. By embodying the values of the kingdom they become signs and anticipations of the new creation that is dawning in Jesus Christ.

THE CHURCH AND SECULAR SOCIETY

Only a naive biblicism, however, could lead us to believe that the social mandate of the church can be adequately settled by appealing to the practice of Jesus and his first followers. Concentrating on evangelization and personal discipleship, they did what was urgent for their own day, when the Christian movement was just being launched. The church of New Testament times was very small and had no opportunity to shape the order of secular society. There is evidence, too, that the end of the world was believed to be at hand, so that it would be pointless to plan for its long-term future. But as the church grew larger and as the centuries passed, Christians could not help but assume a measure of responsibility for the social order. Their vision of the good society was bound to make a significant impact on public life and institutions. Christian morality, therefore, took on more evidently social and political dimensions.

With the conversion of the Empire to Christianity and the subsequent collapse of the Empire in the West, the church was drawn into very direct relationships with the political powers. At first the dominant relationship was one of close collaboration bordering on co-option. The emperors used the church to some degree to cement the unity of the Empire under their own authority. Then, as imperial authority and cultural institutions collapsed in Western Europe and North Africa, the church had to move into the vacuum. Churchmen

---

4. Troeltsch, *The Social Teaching of the Christian Churches*, vol. 1 (Chicago: University of Chicago Press, 1981), p. 61.

took on political and cultural responsibilities that would not otherwise have come their way.

Medieval theologians, not finding an adequate basis for political theory in the Scriptures, had recourse to Greek philosophy as an additional source. This combination of revealed and natural wisdom, while it did not enjoy the uncontested authority of dogma, provided a solid intellectual basis for reflection on the scope and limits of human government and on the relations between the spiritual and temporal powers. The papacy tended to make exorbitant claims so as to keep the actions of princes and emperors in line with the interests of religion, but these claims were continually resisted. The nationalism of the sixteenth century put a definitive end to papal claims to domination, at least in most parts of the world, not excepting Europe.

Since the Enlightenment, the church has exercised very little direct political power. Its intervention in the social sphere occurs most prominently through statements that are intended to influence the ideas and behavior of Catholics and other receptive readers. The social teaching of the church, as we understand the term today, dates from the mid-nineteenth century. Responding to the disturbances of 1848, Baron Wilhelm von Ketteler (who was to become Bishop of Mainz two years later) saw both a challenge and an opportunity. "The world will see," he declared, "that to the Catholic Church is reserved the definitive solution of the social question; for the State, with all its legislative machinery, has not the power to solve it."[5]

In *Rerum novarum* (1891) Pope Leo XIII initiated what has developed into a long series of social encyclicals. These letters, addressing urgent problems of the political and economic order, propound a social philosophy grounded in universal ethical principles that are deemed consonant with, though not directly derivable from, revelation. This social philosophy is in many respects an updating of that devised by Thomas Aquinas and other medieval theologians.

This response on the official level, dealing directly with social questions, may be seen as a supplement to, rather than a replacement of, the indirect impact on society of the church's traditional ministries. Through its proclamation of Christ and the kingdom, the church holds up a vision of ultimate religious meaning, and those

---

5. Von Ketteler, quoted by Edward Cahill in "The Catholic Social Movement: Historical Aspects," reprinted in *Official Catholic Social Teaching*, Readings in Moral Theology No. 5, ed. Charles E. Curran and Richard A. McCormick (New York: Paulist Press, 1986), p. 9.

who accept this vision take a distinctive attitude toward life and death, pleasure and pain, truth and falsehood, wealth and poverty, power and weakness. The Christian view of life serves as a kind of leaven that, through the lives of committed believers, gradually penetrates and transforms the entire social environment. In a Christianized culture, institutions such as schools and hospitals, prisons, slavery, and even war are progressively infused with a spirit of mercy and with loving esteem for each individual. Scholarly studies can trace how the legal and political institutions of Christian countries, including feudalism and common law, came to be imbued with Christian values. Christian faith, it is sometimes contended, has "helped to supply the ideas through which democratic capitalism has emerged in history."[6] Even anti-Christian movements such as Marxian and Saint-Simonian socialism would not have taken the forms they did had it not been for the social ferment of the gospel.

This does not of course mean that the organization and practice of public life in the West were at any time totally Christian. The old Adam with his selfishness survives in every believer, and many who have gone by the name of Christian have failed to put the gospel into practice. The church has never been able to do away with sin and unfaithfulness in its own members, let alone in society at large. The growing secularization of society since the Enlightenment has put additional barriers in the path of Christianization. But obstacles such as these do not absolve the church from the task of striving to accomplish the evangelization of social institutions.

TWO STYLES OF MAGISTERIAL TEACHING

While there is always a danger of exaggerating the contrasts, it seems undeniable that there has been a shift in the style of Catholic social teaching since the early social encyclicals of Leo XIII and Pius XI. The new style began to emerge with John XXIII, but is most clearly displayed in Vatican II's Pastoral Constitution, *Gaudium et spes;* in Paul VI's letter on the eightieth anniversary of *Rerum novarum, Octogesima Adveniens* (1971); and in the document of the Synod of Bishops, *Justice in the World* (1971).

The earlier style of official teaching made a rather sharp cleavage between the church, as a supernatural society, and the world, as the province of natural law. The church was directly con-

---

6. Michael Novak, *The Spirit of Democratic Capitalism* (New York: Simon & Schuster, 1982), p. 334.

cerned with supernatural salvation but as a teacher of virtue it could authentically interpret the natural law, which was normative for secular behavior. The church, moreover, was seen as a strictly hierarchical society in which the pope and bishops issued doctrinal pronouncements and practical directives that were to be transmitted in the church by parish priests and applied in the world by the laity. The style of speech, accordingly, was didactic and authoritative.

In more recent teaching it seems possible to detect an anthropological shift. All human beings, since they have the same transcendent destiny, are understood as possessing the same basic inviolability and therefore as being essentially equal (*LG*, 32). Each, moreover, is ruled by personal conscience, even in religious matters (*DH*, 1; *GS*, 41). In view of their intrinsic dignity, all should, as far as possible, participate responsibly in social and political life (*GS*, 73). Likewise, the active participation of the faithful is appropriate within the church (*SC*, 14). Ordained ministry is seen not as a dignity but as a call to humble service (*PO*, 3 and 15).

This anthropological shift affects the church-world relationship. The church, rather than being a *societas perfecta* alongside of the secular state, is seen as a pilgrim people, subject to the vicissitudes of history, and sharing in the concerns and destiny of the whole human race (*GS*, 1). The church is linked to the world as the sacrament of universal unity (*LG*, 1), a sign and safeguard of the transcendence of the human person (*GS*, 76), a defender of authentic human rights (*GS*, 41). In a dynamically evolving world (*GS*, 4), social and political liberation pertains integrally to the process of redemption, and hence is not foreign to the mission of the church. The 1971 Synod of Bishops went so far as to declare that "Action on behalf of justice and participation in the transformation of the world fully appear to us as a constitutive dimension of the preaching of the Gospel, or, in other words, of the church's mission for the redemption of the human race and its liberation from every oppressive situation" (*JW*, 6). The church's concern for human solidarity, peace, and justice, therefore, is not confined to the sphere of supernatural salvation in a life beyond.

These anthropological and ecclesiological shifts demanded revisions in the church's methodology and in its official style of speaking about social questions. Beginning with *Gaudium et spes* one notices a much more empirical methodology, which includes a careful phenomenology of the present situation. The magisterium increasingly recognizes the need for its teaching to be adapted to the various situations in different parts of the world. Thus Paul VI in *Octogesima Adveniens* declares,

In the face of such widely varying situations it is difficult for us to utter a unified message and to put forward a solution which has universal validity. Such is not our ambition, nor is it our mission. It is up to the Christian communities to analyze with objectivity the situation which is proper to their own country, to shed on it the light of the Gospel's unalterable words and to draw principles of reflection, norms of judgment and directives for action from the social teaching of the Church. . . . It is up to these Christian communities, with the help of the Holy Spirit, in communion with the bishops who hold responsibility and in dialogue with other Christian brethren and all men of good will, to discern the options and commitments which are called for. (*OA*, 4)

In its efforts to interpret the "signs of the times" and to discern the appropriate response of Christians to concrete situations, the church is beginning to speak in a more tentative style. Maintaining an open dialogue among its own members and with other communities, it strives to be receptive to criticism and to submit its teaching to continuous revision. Infallibility, which retains its value for strictly dogmatic statements, is deemed inapplicable to the new style of social teaching.

THE UNITED STATES EPISCOPAL CONFERENCE: METHODOLOGY

Not a few regional churches have taken up the challenge that seemed to be contained in the documents I have cited. The Latin American bishops, in their general conferences at Medellín (1968) and Puebla (1979), attempted to articulate a social doctrine adapted to their own time and situation. The United States bishops, who had begun issuing policy statements as early as 1919, developed a more elaborate technique, notably in their two recent pastoral letters *The Challenge of Peace* (1983) and *Economic Justice for All* (1986).

From the standpoint of methodology, the introduction to *The Challenge of Peace* merits careful attention. The bishops distinguish three types of statement in their own document: declarations of universal moral principles that are presumably accessible to all through reason and conscience, reiterations of Catholic social teaching as found in papal and conciliar documents, and prudential applications of these principles and teachings to the particular circumstances of the contemporary situation. The bishops are very modest regarding the authority of these applications:

When making applications of these principles we realize—

and we wish readers to recognize—that prudential judgments are involved based on specific circumstances which can change or which can be interpreted differently by people of good will (e.g., the treatment of "no first use"). However, the moral judgments that we make in specific cases, while not binding in conscience, are to be given serious attention and consideration by Catholics as they determine whether their moral judgments are consistent with the Gospel. (*CP*, 10)

Similar disclaimers of obligatory force are enunciated in the pastoral on the economy. The "illustrative topics," say the bishops, are "intended to exemplify the interaction of moral values and economic issues in our day, not to encompass all such values and issues." The document is "an attempt to foster a serious moral analysis leading to a more just economy" (*EJ*, 133).

In the following paragraph (*EJ*, 134), the bishops are even more explicit:

In focusing on some of the central economic issues and choices in American life in the light of moral principles, we are aware that the movement from principle to policy is complex and difficult and that although moral values are essential in determining public policies, they do not dictate specific solutions. They must interact with empirical data, with historical, social, and political realities, and with competing demands on limited resources. The soundness of our prudential judgments depends not only on the moral force of our principles, but also on the accuracy of our information and the validity of our assumptions.

This methodological section concludes with an important paragraph on the authority of the pastoral's positions on policy issues:

Our judgments and recommendations on specific economic issues, therefore, do not carry the same moral authority as our statements of universal moral principles and formal church teaching; the former are related to circumstances which can change or which can be interpreted differently by people of good will. We expect and welcome debate on our specific policy recommendations. Nevertheless, we want our statements on these matters to be given serious consideration by Catholics as they determine whether their own moral judgments are consistent with the Gospel and with Catholic social teaching. We believe that differences on complex economic questions should be expressed in a spirit of mutual respect and open dialogue. (*EJ*, 135)

Open dialogue was actually built into the process by which the two pastorals were hammered out. The bishops held extensive hearings in different parts of the country with experts of various points of view. They published preliminary drafts, invited criticisms, and thoroughly revised their own work several times in the light of the feedback. Thus the final statement, although issued in the name of the bishops, was produced with a great deal of input from others, including the laity. The names of the staff, consultants, and witnesses were published. This represents a major development since 1931, when the collaboration of Oswald von Nell-Breuning, S.J., in the drafting of the encyclical *Quadragesimo anno* was kept in absolute secret, which he was not allowed to share even with his provincial and local superiors.[7]

PRINCIPLES AND APPLICATIONS

Although there are methodological innovations in the recent pastorals, leading to a different style and degree of authority, it would be an oversimplification to imagine that the new method has been substituted for the old. The traditional style of Catholic social teaching remains in place and is illustrated by *Laborem exercens* (1981), an encyclical issued by John Paul II on the ninetieth anniversary of *Rerum novarum*. The American bishops do not seek to distance themselves from the Catholic tradition of social doctrine, which they explicitly invoke and build into their own analysis. In *The Challenge of Peace* the bishops accept and apply the just war doctrine with its norms, such as just cause, competent authority, right intention, last resort, probability of success, proportionality, and discrimination. In *Economic Justice for All* they invoke principles such as respect for human dignity, the common good, the preferential option for the poor, active participation, and subsidiarity. In all of this they rely on the developing body of social teaching contained in Vatican II's *Gaudium et spes* and in the papal encyclicals.

The general principles of social ethics contained in the two pastoral letters aroused only moderate opposition and were to a great extent accepted by the critics. Michael Novak in his alternative peace pastoral, *Moral Clarity in the Nuclear Age*, makes use of almost precisely the same just war principles as the bishops, though his applications are quite different. Another critic, Ernest Fortin, while likewise adhering to the traditional just war doctrine, suggests that

---

7. Von Nell-Breuning, "The Drafting of *Quadragesimo Anno*," reprinted in *Official Catholic Social Teaching*, pp. 60-68.

the bishops give an excessively juridical or legalistic interpretation to that doctrine, depriving statesmen of the flexibility required to meet unique and unpredictable contingencies.[8]

The criticism of the social principles in the economics pastoral was likewise rather mild. According to Peter Berger, critics such as William Simon and Michael Novak, although they come to very different conclusions about specifics, make use of the same ethical presuppositions and the same method of reasoning as the bishops.[9] To be precise, one would have to add that Simon and Novak, in their "lay letter" *Toward the Future* and in their report *Liberty and Justice for All* (5 November 1986), differ from the bishops in their interpretation of economic rights. They also fault the bishops for failing to emphasize liberty as a crucial factor in social justice.

Controversy about the two pastorals has centered less on the principles than on the practical applications, for which the bishops themselves claimed little authority. Regarding the peace pastoral, the critics question, for instance, whether limited nuclear war is in fact an impossibility and whether the United States could prudently commit itself never to use nuclear weapons unless such weapons had first been used by the enemy. With regard to the economy, there is disagreement about whether the minimum wage should be further increased (*EJ*, 197), whether affirmative action should be more rigorously enforced (*EJ*, 73, 167, 199), whether the tax system should be structured according to the principle of progressivity (*EJ*, 202), and whether responsibility for welfare programs should be shifted from the states to the federal government (*EJ*, 213). It is occasionally objected that the two pastorals are inconsistent. Can one demand greater reliance on conventional weapons (*CP*, 216) while the other calls for a sharp reduction in appropriations for defense (*EJ*, 148, 289, 320)? These are only a sampling of the many detailed criticisms that have been and are being made.

As we have seen, the bishops do not claim that their practical applications follow inevitably from their convictions as men of faith. They recognize that intelligent and committed Christians may disagree with their concrete policy positions. But the coherence of their document depends upon the existence of some link between the principles and the applications. Otherwise the bishops could scarcely claim in *The Challenge of Peace* that their contribution is pastoral

---

8. Fortin, "Theological Reflections on a Pastoral Letter," *Catholicism in Crisis* 1 (July 1983): 9-12, especially p. 10.

9. Berger, "Can the Bishops Help the Poor?" in *Challenge and Response: Critiques of the Catholic Bishops' Draft Letter on the Economy* (Washington: Ethics and Public Policy Center, 1985), p. 63.

rather than primarily technical or political (*CP* summary, ii), nor could they maintain in *Economic Justice for All* that "We write as pastors, not public officials. We speak as moral teachers, not economic technicians" (*EJ*, 7). The claim is implicitly made that the bishops' policy positions are more in line with the gospel and with Catholic social philosophy than alternative positions would be.

We may readily admit that people's moral and spiritual attitudes, including their faith outlook, affect what they see and understand about the world in which they live. Selfishness and prejudice can blind people to facts, problems, and solutions. A deep personal conversion to the gospel can lead to greater discernment in human questions that touch on the order of religion and morality. If individuals can thus derive wisdom from their faith, the same is even more true of a religious community, which is the bearer of corporate moral insights built up through the accumulated reflection of many generations. The bishops could perhaps claim that their situation within the community of faith and the tradition of Christian reflection gives them a privileged sensitivity to the moral and religious aspects of the current policy debate.

Yet there are grounds for questioning such a claim. If commitment to the gospel gave the kind of insight embodied in the policy recommendations of the two pastorals, one would expect that evangelical Christians would be the chief supporters of the bishops and that agnostic liberals would be the leading opponents. But this does not appear to be the case; if anything, the opposite is true.

The authors of the pastorals might reply, of course, that most evangelical Christians, not being formed in the Catholic tradition, have a distorted view of the gospel. Does the Catholic tradition, then, account for the difference between the supporters and the opponents of the bishops? This seems hardly to be so, since many of the bishops' policy positions are acceptable to large numbers of nonreligious liberals but not to many traditionally oriented Catholics. It may also be noted that the peace pastoral, especially in its second draft, met with rather negative reception in Western European ecclesiastical circles. Even after it was amended to avoid open conflict with recent papal teaching, the pastoral still stood in some tension with analogous documents on deterrence issued by episcopal authorities in Belgium, France, Germany, England, and Wales. The Holy See, and especially the Cardinal Secretary of State, are still seeking to iron out the inner-Catholic disagreements with regard to the stockpiling and threatened use of nuclear weapons.[10]

---

10. See Francis X. Winters, "After Tension, Détente: A Continuing

Many critics complain that the true sources of the applications in the pastoral on peace are not to be found in authoritative Catholic teaching but rather in liberal American academic circles. George Weigel, for instance, asserts that

> However difficult it may be to find the bishops' approach clearly implied by the norms the bishops establish, it is rather easy to find that part of the political culture in which the bishops' views have great resonance—and that is in a fairly narrow band of what we might call the "institutional arms control fraternity."[11]

The net effect of the pastoral, Weigel concludes, is to "lend the weight of their [the bishops'] public credibility to factions within the already existing argument"—factions that "seem to have had an inordinate impact on the bishops' own reflections."[12]

Similar charges have been leveled at the economics pastoral. Although the bishops speak with great circumspection and repeatedly praise free enterprise, subsidiarity, and "mediating institutions," they are accused of relying too much on government programs and even of adopting "a preferential option for the state" (Simon and Novak). Novak attributes this flaw to the influence of the Catholic tradition in social thought stemming from Wilhelm von Ketteler and Heinrich Pesch. Acknowledging that this tradition has heavily influenced the official teaching of the popes, Novak believes that the defect can be remedied. Just as American Catholicism was the chief catalyst in bringing about a shift in the official Catholic teaching on religious liberty at Vatican II, so too, he maintains, the American experience of capitalism may stimulate a new advance in Catholic social and economic teaching:

> Through the lonely pioneering work of John Courtney Murray, S.J., the experience of religious liberty under democratic

---

Chronicle of European Episcopal Views on Nuclear Deterrence," *Theological Studies* 45 (1984): 343-51.

11. Weigel, "The Bishops' Pastoral Letter and the American Political Culture: Who Was Influencing Whom?" in *Peace in a Nuclear Age: The Bishops' Pastoral Letter in Perspective*, ed. Charles J. Reid, Jr. (Washington: Catholic University of America, 1986), p. 181.

12. Weigel, "The Bishops' Pastoral Letter," p. 187. Charles N. Luttwak writes, "When I read the pastoral letter I see, before me, one of those 'faddish' documents that are produced by people who succumb to surrounding social pressures and accept opinions not their own" ("Catholics and the Bomb: The Perspective of a Non-Catholic Strategist," in *Peace in a Nuclear Age*, p. 169). A group of seven essays at the beginning of *Peace in a Nuclear Age* reflects on *The Challenge of Peace* in relation to the Catholic theological tradition, including the Bible.

capitalism finally, after so much resistance, enriched the patrimony of the Catholic church. So also, I hope, arguments in favor of "the natural system of liberty" will one day enrich the church's conception of political economy.[13]

Novak is correct, I believe, in saying that the bishops are indebted to a long Catholic tradition that looks primarily to government action to remedy malfunctionings in the economy and that that tradition may be overly dependent on precapitalist and anticapitalist models. Other critics assert somewhat contemptuously that the bishops are "following in the well-worn footsteps of a major segment of official mainline Protestantism"[14] and that although "we now have a generation of experience with liberal social programs . . . the bishops appear to have just discovered them."[15] These particular complaints, besides exaggerating the partisanship of *Economic Justice for All*, fail to recognize that the American Catholic bishops have been pressing for reform of the economy by government intervention ever since 1919 and that the Holy See has always tended to distrust free enterprise.

TOO SPECIFIC? GROUNDS FOR CAUTION

The fundamental question in my opinion is not whether the bishops rely on secular sources for their ideas or even whether their policy recommendations are correct, but rather whether they ought to give detailed answers in controverted areas such as nuclear policy, taxation, welfare programs, and the like. Ernest Fortin suggests that they should not:

> These are the types of issues that divide political parties and they are issues over which well informed and well intentioned elected officials and citizens are bound to disagree. . . . When the bulk of the Christian tradition is not clearly on one side, one should think twice before affixing the seal of divine approval on any one of them.[16]

---

13. Novak, *The Spirit of Democratic Capitalism*, p. 28.

14. Berger, "Can the Bishops Help the Poor," in *Challenge and Response*, p. 63.

15. Charles Krauthammer, "Perils of the Prophet Motive," in *Challenge and Response*, p. 52.

16. Fortin, "Catholic Social Teaching and the Economy," *Catholicism in Crisis* 3 (January 1985): 43. A similar line of criticism is developed by J. Brian Benestad in "The Bishops' Pastoral Letter on the Economy: Theological Criteria and Criticisms," *Notre Dame Journal of Law, Ethics, and Public Policy* 2 (1985): 161-77.

The case in favor of making specific applications has been ably argued by J. Bryan Hehir. Moral principles, he contends, must be incarnated in the fabric of a social problem in order for their significance and illuminative power to appear. There is a risk "in stating principles so abstractly that all acknowledge them, then proceed to widely divergent conclusions while claiming support of the principle." He goes on to say in summation, "I am persuaded from following the commentary on both pastoral letters of the U.S. bishops that neither would have found their way to the center of the national policy debate if they had not pursued basic principles through to contingent but concrete conclusions."[17]

It is undoubtedly true that the bishops gain more national attention by taking specific positions on contentious issues, but when one considers the price of such specificity, it would seem that good arguments can be made for restraint.

In drawing up pastorals such as those on peace and on the economy, the bishops make an enormous investment of time and energy in questions that are also being dealt with, from a very similar perspective, by a variety of foundations, public interest groups, and educational institutions. Is it justified for them to go so far afield when many ecclesiastical matters, for which the bishops have inescapable responsibility, are crying out for greater attention? The impression is given that the bishops are more at ease in criticizing the performance of secular governments than in shouldering their own responsibilities in the church. Few of the American bishops today enjoy a great reputation for their mastery of theology, liturgy, or spiritual direction, yet many of them are known for their views on politics and the economy.

When the bishops devote so much attention to worldly affairs, they can unwittingly give the impression that what is truly important in their eyes is not the faith or holiness that leads to everlasting life but rather the structuring of human society to make the world more habitable. The church has in the past managed to convey the conviction that poverty and worldly suffering are only relative evils, because the wretched of the earth, if they are pure in heart, are loved by God and destined for eternal blessedness. Conversely it has conveyed to the rich and prosperous the warning that if they become proud and use their riches selfishly they must fear divine retribution. Such, as we have seen, was the message of Jesus. The appeal to

---

17. Hehir, "Church-State and Church-World: The Ecclesiological Implications," *Proceedings of the Catholic Theological Society of America* 41 (1986): 69, 70.

sociopolitical analysis in recent episcopal teaching, coupled with an almost total lack of eschatological reference, gives the impression that the church's pastors have little confidence in its spiritual patrimony. It can be scarcely surprising if a church that gives such high priority to politics and economics suffers a serious decline in conversions and in priestly and religious vocations.

While there is no doubt that an individual bishop may be well versed in questions of military strategy or economics, the publication of elaborate and highly technical conference statements on nuclear weapons and the economy arouses suspicions that the bishops are exceeding their competence. The entire membership of a national conference can hardly make itself responsible for the details of its own documents, drawn up as they are by staff and committees. When questioned by journalists shortly after issuing their peace pastoral, a number of bishops admitted that they did not really understand certain recommendations contained in their own letter.

Although the policy positions in these documents are put forth as following (albeit contingently) from the moral and religious principles of Catholic Christianity, the suspicion remains that these positions are heavily indebted to current theories about the efficacy of certain means (such as conventional weapons or government welfare programs) to achieve goals that are shared by practically everyone (peace, prosperity). For the soundness of these theories there are no biblical or theological warrants. Can the bishops properly claim that in making such recommendations they are speaking as spiritual leaders rather than as citizens who accept certain views about political and social science?

Papal documents have recognized "a legitimate variety of possible options" inasmuch as "the same Christian faith can lead to different commitments" (*OA*, 50). By taking particular options and by sponsoring elaborate programs to disseminate their pastoral teaching, the bishops seem to restrict the options open to Catholics. Although the bishops are far from excommunicating persons who gainsay their policy statements, a Catholic who wishes to take a stand different from that of the national hierarchy will inevitably feel somewhat alienated from, or marginalized in, the church.

To the extent that dissent from pastoral letters of this type is openly tolerated, factionalism is encouraged in the church. Catholics take up the cry first heard in opposition to Pope John XXIII, "*Mater, si; magistra, no!*" The spirit of criticism and dissent thus unleashed can scarcely be prevented from spreading to strictly religious matters in which the bishops have unquestionable authority in the church. By speaking out on issues of a secular character, bishops undermine their authority in areas that clearly fall within the scope of their mission. One conservative lay critic writes, "Forgive me, fathers, but aren't you squandering your moral capital?"[18]

As the official church moves from the realm of social teaching to that of concrete policy positions, it becomes entangled in the ambiguities of mundane politics. Practically speaking, for example, one may be faced with the choice of either supporting health benefits that include entitlements to sterilization and abortions or allowing all such programs to be defeated. In practical politics one frequently has to accept compromises. By taking partisan positions on current issues (whether in pastoral letters or in other occasional statements), a bishops' conference can easily fall into the kind of political pragmatism that has proved so harmful to the church's moral standing in traditionally Catholic countries. It is one of the blessings of the American system that the church has rarely endorsed particular political parties or candidates for office. But as it moves into the public policy realm, the risks of entanglement increase.

When concrete instructions are issued by the hierarchy on issues of a social and political character, the question arises whether the laity are being deprived of their distinctive responsibility. Vatican II asserted that the renewal of the temporal order is the special responsibility of laity (AA, 7) and that the clergy should not be expected to offer concrete solutions to complex secular questions (GS, 43). The 1971 Synod of Bishops stated starkly, "It does not belong to the church, insofar as she is a religious and hierarchical community, to offer concrete solutions in the social, economic, and political spheres for justice in the world" (JW, 37).

Already in 1977 a group of American Catholics expressed anxiety over the increasing clericalization of the social apostolate. In their "Chicago Declaration of Concern" they protested that

> During the last decade especially, many priests have acted as if the primary responsiblility of the Church for uprooting injustice, ending wars, and defending human rights rested with them as ordained ministers. As a result, they bypassed the laity to pursue social causes on their own rather than enabling lay Christians to shoulder their own responsibility. These priests and religious have sought to impose their own agendas for the world upon the laity.[19]

---

18. Philip F. Lawler, "Squandering Moral Capital," in *Challenge and Response*, p. 74.
19. "Declaration of Concern: On Devaluing the Laity," *Origins* 7 (29 December 1977): 441.

J. Brian Benestad, referring to this and other texts, comments that the American bishops, by frequently issuing policy statements through their conference and its committees, "have effectively adopted the role of the outsider as the model of political action."[20] I agree that it is generally best for the concrete applications of Christian social teaching to be made by laypeople who are regularly involved in secular affairs, especially those of the laity who are specialists in the pertinent disciplines.

GROUNDS FOR SPECIFICITY

From this inventory of disadvantages it does not follow that popes and bishops should never issue concrete directives about social and political questions, but only that they should move cautiously in this field. The United States bishops have exercised commendable restraint, notably in their economics pastoral. They have drawn a clear line of demarcation between their doctrinal teaching and their policy recommendations; they have phrased those recommendations modestly and have explicitly pointed out that the particular policy recommendations are not binding in conscience on those who honestly disagree.

Although I have reservations about the wisdom of certain policy statements that have been issued by the United States episcopal conference in recent years, I do not hold that the bishops should be confined to speaking in airy generalities. I can think of several reasons why ecclesiastical authorities might find it advisable to propose specific policies in the name of the church (rather than simply as citizens or civil officials).

First, they might find it necessary as teachers to indicate how their doctrinal principles might work out in practice, so that the illuminative power of those principles (to repeat Bryan Hehir's term) might more clearly appear. Such concreteness, however, could be achieved by hypothetical examples without it being affirmed that the example is necessarily well chosen. Even for those who reject the specific policies endorsed in *Economic Justice for All*, the applications can serve as valuable illustrations of how a Christian might propose to bring the economy into closer conformity with Catholic social teaching.

Second, the authorities might have reasons for pointing out that certain applications are so obvious that no room is left for reasonable

---

20. Benestad, *The Pursuit of a Just Social Order* (Washington: Ethics and Public Policy Center, 1982), p. 114.

disagreement among properly instructed Christians. Whatever may have been true in the past, it seems undeniable that institutions such as slavery and torture are no longer acceptable. It may also be possible to say with confidence that a given act of aggression violates the criteria for a just war. An affirmative judgment that a given war ought to be waged, as positively satisfying all the criteria, is far more difficult to reach.

Third, there can be urgent situations in which it is imperative for Catholics to act in unison in order to prevent an opportunity from being lost. For example, the Filipino bishops may well have been justified when in February 1986 they denounced the irregularities of the presidential election. Or, to give another illustration, the bishops of some country might wish to support one of several acceptable antiabortion bills in order to prevent Catholics from being so divided that all such bills would be defeated. Since the bishops are the only persons who can effectively direct the Catholic community, they must give moral leadership when united action is necessary. Practical directives of this kind should, however, be clearly distinguished from Catholic social teaching.

A number of recent theologians would wish to add that the official leadership of the church should intervene prophetically in certain concrete situations in which there were not sufficient doctrinal warrants for a clear magisterial teaching. As an example, Edward Schillebeeckx suggests issuing a directive that certain large estates in a particular region should be broken up, if necessary, by expropriation. In taking such action, he holds, the official church, functioning under the charismatic guidance of the Spirit, could speak out decisively. Even though the directive in question lay beyond the scope of the church's teaching office, it would merit the obedience due to the church's pastoral function.[21]

In answer to this proposal I can only say that if the hierarchy is indeed moved by the spirit of prophecy, it ought to speak out boldly even on a concrete issue of politics or economics. But I hesitate to make a rule out of the unforeseeable interventions of the Spirit. I would think that charismatic assistance might appropriately be given to the political rather than to the ecclesiastical authorities in a case of this kind. In any case I would want rather clear assurances that purportedly prophetic utterances about contingent secular issues were in fact divinely prompted.

---

21. Schillebeeckx, *God: The Future of Man* (New York: Sheed & Ward, 1968), p. 163. Somewhat analogous ideas, possibly influenced by Schillebeeckx, are advanced by Karl Rahner in *The Shape of the Church to Come* (New York: Seabury, 1974), pp. 76-81.

REFLECTIONS ON THE ERASMUS LECTURE

The convergences and divergences between my paper and Peter Berger's Erasmus Lecture are many and various. To facilitate the discussion I shall here attempt to select a few issues from the advance text sent to me.

The first half of the lecture raises some very interesting questions about the sociology of contemporary American Christianity. The main thesis, as I understand it, is that the social activism of the clergy is a consequence of the rise of a new knowledge class that stands to gain (in certain unspecified ways) from a shift of power from business to government and from a deemphasis on military power in foreign policy. Berger speaks in general terms without indicating to what extent he regards this analysis as a key to the interpretation of contemporary Catholic social teaching.

Influenced in part by Berger, some conservative Catholics have contended that the National Conference of Catholic Bishops has been manipulated by this power-hungry elite. Thus Berger's type of ideological critique is being used in some quarters to discredit the bishops' pastoral letters as the work of a subversive class. It apparently does not occur to the critics that their own hermeneutic of suspicion can be turned against them. In the words of Dennis McCann,

> those who traffic in the profoundly modernist strategy of stressing ideological critiques like the New Class Theory will always be vulnerable to having the tables turned. Isn't the recent effort of neoconservative intellectuals to discredit the bishops' pastoral letter on the economy itself the most dramatic instance of an entrenched New Class conspiring to maintain its passing hegemony in public policy debate?[22]

The "new class" thesis, with appropriate qualifications, had a modicum of validity with regard to American Catholicism in the 1970s, but whatever power the new knowledge class may have had with the bishops crested, I would say, about a decade ago. Ever since the Detroit Call to Action Conference (1976) the bishops have tried to be sensitive to the concerns of mainstream Catholics. Their own personal positions on many issues, such as family life, abortion, and the ERA, align them more closely with the old than with the new middle class. Their reservations about big business and heavy arsenals arise from a combination of factors, not excluding the teach-

---

22. McCann, "New Face on an Old Criticism," *Commonweal* 113 (26 December 1986), Supplement Marking the Tenth Anniversary of a Call to Action, p. 13.

ing of Jesus and the previous pronouncements of popes and councils. It would be a gross caricature to depict them, or even their principal advisers, as having "moved into strong, sometimes virulent opposition to key American institutions and values" (Berger's essay, p. 5 herein). Some neoconservatives have greatly exaggerated both the radicalism of the bishops and the influence of the supposedly sinister new knowledge class.

My differences with Berger show up mainly in the theological section of his lecture (or at least of the draft available to me). He is surely not an Erasmian. How typical he is of Lutheranism I must leave it to others to judge. He certainly echoes many Lutheran themes—the church as herald of the gospel, the gospel as a solace to anxious consciences, justification by faith alone "without works of the law," the separation of the two kingdoms, and the vitiation of all human effort by sin. Since my theological perspectives on all five of these themes differ from Berger's, I have some problems about the ways in which he applies these themes to Christian social action.

1. Berger presents the church almost exclusively as proclaimer of the gospel. That is certainly an important task, but the church, I would contend, must also be viewed as a community that attempts to respond to the gospel by worship and works of love. The social teaching of the church, while in some sense derivative from the gospel, is more closely related to the responding phase of its life than to the proclamatory.[23] Thus the herald model of the church, while useful up to a point, is simply inadequate for dealing with the whole question of its social responsibility.[24]

---

23. My distinction between proclamation and response might seem to diverge from the Synod of 1971, which spoke on behalf of justice as "a constitutive dimension of the preaching of the gospel." This much-debated definition was toned down at the 1974 Synod, which in its working paper spoke only of an "intrinsic connection" between evangelization and human promotion. Summarizing the results of the 1974 Synod, Paul VI in *Evangelii nuntiandi* (1975) was content to assert, "Between evangelization and human advancement—development and liberation —there are in fact profound links" inasmuch as the plan of creation cannot be dissociated from the plan of redemption (*EN*, 31).

Charles M. Murphy, after a detailed review of the debate, concludes that the relationship between proclamation and social action may best be understood in terms of the dialectic between gift and task. Evangelization indicates what God is doing, but "the human response is indispensable as the necessary response to the divine initiative" ("Action for Justice as Constitutive of the Preaching of the Gospel: What Did the 1971 Synod Mean?" *Theological Studies* 44 [1983]: 310).

24. On the "herald" model of the church, see chapter 5 of my *Models of the Church* (Garden City, N.Y.: Doubleday, 1974).

2. When he speaks of the gospel, Berger regularly focuses on the solace and consolation that it brings. This, too, is an important consideration, but woefully incomplete. The consolations, I would maintain, are reserved to those who accept the challenge of the gospel, sincerely seeking to amend their ways and obey the commandments of Christ. Faith, in the sense of trust, would not be a sufficient response to the gospel.

3. In the main body of my paper I have already dealt at some length with the question of good works. Paul, as I read him, is as emphatic as Jesus and James in insisting that one must not only hear the words of Christ but also put them into practice (Matt. 7:24-27; Luke 6:46-49; Rom. 2:13; James 1:22-25). Paul may at times insist on the insufficiency of the Mosaic law, with its ritual and dietary prescriptions, but he leaves no room for doubt that Christians are obliged to "bear one another's burdens and so fulfill the law of Christ" (Gal. 6:2). To proclaim the gospel without requiring righteous behavior would be truly to proclaim "another gospel."

4. Berger makes a sharper dichotomy between the "two kingdoms" than I think proper. His statements about avoiding "political agendas" can be defended if understood in a certain sense, but his language is too undifferentiated for clarity. When is an agenda political? What should the church have to say about slavery, torture, genocide, concentration camps, and gas chambers? If there were a neat separation between the religious, moral, and political spheres, things might be a lot simpler than they are. But the spheres overlap, and for this reason the church cannot totally divorce itself from the political sphere.

5. Doubtless it is true, as Berger says, that "all our notions of justice are fallible and finally marred by sin." Sin and finitude leave their mark on every human conception. But does this acknowledgment relieve Christians of their responsibility to struggle for justice in society? If so, I think it would also absolve them from the obligation to proclaim the gospel, since, as fallen creatures, they understand it deficiently. In both proclamation and performance, I submit, we are bound to do what we can with the help of grace, and leave the rest to God.

"Our projects in this world," says Berger, "almost never yield the results we intend." No doubt, I would say; but sometimes we build better than we know. God can prosper our endeavors. And if they turn out badly, the moral value of our effort depends more on our intentions than on our actual achievements. The intentions of our heart are manifest to God's eyes, and he who sees in secret will be our judge and our rewarder.

In spite of our apparent differences, Peter Berger and I can perhaps unite on the platform drawn up at Hartford in 1975. He was a prime mover in initially drafting the "Appeal for Theological Affirmation," and I was a participant in the final editing of the text.[25]

The perceptive reader will have noticed that my emphases in this essay in many ways reflect positions taken in the Hartford Appeal. Like the other Hartford signatories, I deplore the politicization of the gospel and the tendency to equate the kingdom of God with the results of human efforts to build a just society. I insist on the utter transcendence of the kingdom and on the primary duty of the church to proclaim the gospel of eternal life. Such proclamation alone can liberate men and women from captivity to inner-worldly values and forces.

I maintain with Hartford that God is to be worshiped because of who he is and not for the sake of human self-realization. With Hartford I deny that "an emphasis on God's transcendence is at least a hindrance to, and perhaps incompatible with, Christian social concern and action" (Theme 11). I assert, likewise, that "the Church must denounce oppressors, help to liberate the oppressed, and seek to heal human misery" (Theme 10). "Because of confidence in God's reign . . . Christians must participate fully in the struggle against oppressive and dehumanizing structures and their manifestations in racism, war, and economic exploitation" (Theme 11).

The whole problem is how to participate in these endeavors without embroiling the church in partisan politics. Where the sense of the transcendent becomes enfeebled, the church, in attempting to address social concerns, simply reduplicates what a multitude of secular agencies are also doing. It loses the capacity to speak a healing and transforming word. For the church to make its proper contribution it must remind the world that there is more to life than politics and that "the form of this world is passing away" (1 Cor. 7:31; cf. 1 John 2:17). As a general rule, faithfulness to Jesus will incline the ecclesiastical authorities to avoid entanglement in economic and political struggles. Jesus himself set the pattern:

> One of the multitude said to him, "Teacher, bid my brother divide the inheritance with me." But he said to him, "Man, who made me a judge or divider over you?" and he said to them, "Take heed, and beware of all covetousness; for a man's life does not consist in the abundance of his possessions." (Luke 12:13-15)

---

25. The text of the Hartford Appeal has been printed in many places. It is available with commentaries by some of the signers in *Against the World for the World: The Hartford Appeal and the Future of American Religion*, ed. Peter L. Berger and Richard John Neuhaus (New York: Seabury, 1976), pp. 1-7.

A "Protestant Constructive Response" to Christian Unbelief

Robert W. Jenson

I

The Center's invitation was one I accepted in haste and contemplated at leisure. The problem is that I am not sure there is a "Protestant" response to the problem of specifically "Christian" unbelief; it may be that the only response Protestantism can make to *this* problem is to become more catholic. Yet it may also be thought that only a Protestant response can be appropriate, since the problem is specifically Protestant. Catholicism generates its own modes of apostasy, but unwitting atheism is a Protestant mode—though it must also be said that much of denominational Roman Catholicism currently seems bent on reenacting it.

In any case, it is, I suppose, incumbent on someone in my position to take responsibility for the Protestant problem and for a response from within it, since I am not presently in communion with Father Dulles and must therefore accept the burden of Protestant history. Moreover, conversation about the assignment with Blanche Jenson has brought me to realize that the recent historical reference of my thinking has been the very hinge of the Protestant problem, since for some years Jonathan Edwards has been the chief interlocutor of my thinking.

Our conference has two announced themes, not at first appraisal identical. It is their crossings that reveal their coherence. If we have an eternal life, we do not ourselves order *it;* rather, we order our life in time by ordering it *to* eternity. Or rather, that is how we used to do it. For belief is precisely the latter ordering, and the sort of unbelief here to be considered is the attempt to perform the former ordering without the latter, and, moreover, to do this within the church itself. And I intend in a moment to overlay these crossings with yet another.

James Turner has established, with remarkable documentary power, that unbelief is an *internal* product of American Protestantism. It has not been his task, in accord with the salutary ascesis of the historian, to diagnose the systematic causes of this productivity. That must be my task. Again, Peter Berger is in my judgment surely correct that for much of mainline Protestantism, political ideology has replaced the gospel. I cannot, however, believe it is dedication to politics that has itself caused the vacuum it fills, since Protestantism can also and just as happily replace belief with quite different substitutes—perhaps most notably cultivation of one "therapy" or another.

Why, theologically-systematically, did Protestant theology and piety react to modernity in the self-destructive fashion that has been in fact characteristic of it? Is there a *theological flaw* in Protestantism that can, at least in part, account for the phenomena Turner and Berger describe? And can the flaw be fixed? In posing such questions, I do not suppose that great historical developments can be compendiously accounted for by the insights and errors that historical agents have entertained; my profession and faith, however, require me to suppose that such explanations are not wholly pointless. Nor do I suppose that coming up with right ideas will by itself reverse a wrong historical development; again, however, both my profession and the faith compel me to think that right ideas are not utterly powerless.

Protestant Christianity has come to proceed, whenever it has a choice to make or a practice to pursue, as if God were not, while remaining fervently dedicated to the Christian religion. But *why*, theologically-systematically, did Protestant theology and piety react to modernism by becoming operationally atheistic? How can religious fervor become so independent of belief in God as Protestant fervor now often is? One as indebted to Karl Barth as am I is, to be sure, tempted simply to say that *religion* is *always* inwardly atheistic, so that there is nothing surprising in the American-Protestant developments. I will resist that temptation.

A priori one might guess that, insofar as ideas are causative in this matter, it would be a flaw in the doctrine of *God* that would account for the phenomena. Is there such a flaw?

II

In order to certify the Protestant character of the proposals I will make, I begin my reflections from two points: a central diagnosis in James Turner's *Without God, without Creed,* and a chief theologoumenon of Jonathan Edwards. At what I take to be a hinge of Turner's book, he describes the division of American Protestantism's relation to God into a cognitive relation bereft of public respectability and an emotive relation respectable as such but bereft of claim to truth. We should note the congruence also of this division with a particular division of time from eternity: it is only as God is present in time that an emotive relation to him can be sustained, and insofar as God is lost in mere atemporality, it is by a putative pure reason that he will for a time still be remembered. It was the beginning of these very divisions, in the described congruence, which Jonathan Edwards noted around himself, which he called "Arminianism," and in the combatting of which he destroyed his career.

III

One of the great feats of modern intellect is contained in Jonathan Edwards's writings during and immediately after the time of the First Awakening: in them, he created a new genre, the "critique" of *religious* "appearances." A 1733 sermon, "A Divine and Supernatural Light," laid out the chief categories he would use, and I will begin with and follow it.

Edwards started with the standard Western analysis of human personhood: we are constituted in intellect on the one hand and will on the other; we are subjects who know objects and choose objects.[1] Therein, of course, he encounters the continuing problem of Western anthropology: if choice is not to be blind and knowledge inhuman— if life, that is to say, is to be orderable—somehow the difference of will and intellect must be transcended.

Every Western thinker has a candidate to be the bridge. Edwards's proposal derives from the deepest spring of his experience and reflection: there is, he says, a sort of consciousness that "is a *sense* of the *beauty*, amiableness or sweetness of a thing; so that the *heart* is sensible of pleasure . . . in the presence of the idea. . . . There is a difference between having a rational judgment that honey is sweet, and having a sense of its sweetness."[2] There can indeed be a purely "notional" judgment *that* something is good, "in which is exercised merely . . . the understanding," but such judgment does not grasp value *as* value. The latter grasp is reserved to "the sense of the heart," in which "the will, or inclination . . . is mainly concerned."[3]

---

1. Edwards, "A Divine and Supernatural Light," Doc., III, Sec., 5.
2. Edwards, "A Divine and Supernatural Light," Doc., I, First, 1. Italics mine.
3. Edwards, "A Divine and Supernatural Light," Doc., I, Sec., 1.

We will miss Edwards's point unless we attend to his choice of adverbs: notional knowledge is "merely" an act of understanding, whereas the "sense" of value is but "mainly" an act of will. The sense of the heart is not mere inclination to or away from an object; it is precisely that the heart is "sensible *of*" (my emphasis) its inclination. For the sense of the heart belongs to that "one thing wherein man differs from brute creatures": "we are always present with ourselves, and have an immediate consciousness of our own actions."[4] The sense of the heart, we may say in the language of thinkers Edwards here anticipated, is a phenomenon of immediate self-awareness; thus it is indeed *awareness*, even "understanding" and "knowledge."[5] It is the knowledge given in that my inclinations are *identified* to me as mine; thus it transcends the difference between knowing and willing.

Edwards was fully intentional in thus locating "sense" as the unity of knowing and willing. In the great treatise *Religious Affections* he wrote that in "spiritual understanding" there can be no "clear distinction made between the two faculties of understanding and will. . . . When the mind is sensible of the sweet beauty . . . of a thing, that implies a sensibleness of sweetness and delight in the presence of the idea of it. And this sensibleness . . . carries in the very notion of it . . . an affect and impression the soul is the subject of, as . . . will."[6]

Thus true religion, according to Edwards, is "a true sense of the divine excellency of the things revealed in the word of God,"[7] of "spiritual good."[8] The believer "has a sense" of "divine and superlative glory"; he "does not merely rationally believe that God is glorious, but he has a sense of the gloriousness of God in his heart."[9]

"This spiritual light is not the suggesting of any new truths"; nor is it characterized by its merely *emotional* quality or intensity. Notional truth about God and appropriate emotion are fully within the possibilities of "mere principles of nature."[10] The religious convictions and emotions of "natural man" are not necessarily notionally incorrect or misdirected. And insofar as they are not, they too are "light" and come from the Spirit; they are gifts of that "common

---

4. Edwards, "That Great Care Is Necessary, Lest We Fall into Some Way of Sin," App., I, 2nd.
5. Edwards, "A Divine and Supernatural Light," Doc., I, Sec., 1.
6. Edwards, *Religious Affections*, Yale Edition, 2:272.
7. Edwards, "A Divine and Supernatural Light," Doc., I, First, 3.
8. Edwards, Yale Edition, 1:142.
9. Edwards, "A Divine and Supernatural Light," Doc., I, Sec., 1.
10. Edwards, "A Divine and Supernatural Light," Doc., I, First, 3-4.

grace" established for the preservation of fallen humanity without which the fall would be into nothingness. Nor is there any reason why the notions and emotions of a natural religionist should not be precisely "those revealed in the word of God"[11]—and indeed, the natural religionists Edwards set out to convert were of course all of that sort. The line between true and merely natural religion does not run between Christian and non-Christian. But where then?

According to Edwards, "Common grace differs from special, in that it influences only by assisting . . . nature," whereas the light "in the mind of a saint" is the activity of the Spirit as "an indwelling vital principle." In the saints, the Spirit acts by "exerting his own nature in the exercise of their faculties."[12] Edwards here makes a dangerous but in my judgment required radicalization of the common doctrine of the indwelling of the Spirit; it is by this radicalized doctrine that he draws the line between religion as a "natural" phenomenon of created life and the saint's distinctive consciousness of God's beauty.

The danger in Edwards's doctrine is signaled by our immediate question: If the Spirit "exerts" *himself* in the activities of saints' "faculties," is not the Spirit then in fact the doer of the saints' works? This very question is the tightrope between what American revivalism was to be and what it might have been had Edwards continued to set its agenda. If the exertions of the Spirit and the works of the saint are identified, this must in practice mean that the convert's agitations are taken directly as the Spirit's presence. It is one of the fatal accidents with which America's theological history is full that the move that voided this consequence for Edwards is among those his untimely death left buried in unpublished drafts.

When Edwards speaks of God, he always means the specifically *triune* God. Nor is his trinitarianism of the sort characteristic of his tradition, which spoke first simply of the one God, in terms adapted to provide the theology of the Enlightenment's "deism," and only thereafter spoke about the way in which this God is *also* triune.[13] As Edwards made the sense of God's beauty our true grasp of his reality, so he made God's beauty the defining character of deity: "God is God, and distinguished from all other beings . . . , chiefly by his divine beauty."[14] Moreover, God's beauty consists in his trinity: "God has appeared glorious to me, on account of the Trinity"; when we see God in his beauty, what we see is "the glorious things of the

---

11. Edwards, "A Divine and Supernatural Light," Doc., I, First, 1.
12. Edwards, "A Divine and Supernatural Light," Doc., I, First, 1.
13. See, for example, William Ames, *Medulla Theologica*, 1.4.31: 6-10.
14. Yale Edition, 2:298.

gospel" as these belong to God's being in that "he subsists in three persons: Father, Son and Holy Ghost."[15]

It is customarily said that Edwards's theology is radically "theocentric," and this is surely true. But Edwards's doctrine will be converted into its contrary if we do not immediately remind ourselves *which* God was the "center"—that is to say, within his proposal of thought, which God was the aesthetically absorbing object. According to Edwards, it is only because God is triune that he can captivate us. God imposes himself by his *beauty*, and "We have shown that one alone cannot be excellent; inasmuch as, in such a case, there can be no consent. Therefore if God is excellent, there must be a plurality in God; otherwise, there can be no consent in him."[16]

Therefore, when Edwards speaks of the Spirit, he means always the Spirit as identified in the doctrine of Trinity. Insofar as we "naturally" grasp reality by the heart's sense, this is the work of the Creator Spirit, precisely in his particularity over against the other triune "persons" and in accord with the inner-triune "relations" by which God is Spirit at all: "For the Spirit . . . is . . . the Author of our capacity of . . . having a sense of heart of natural good or evil. . . . It was especially the work of the Spirit of God in creating . . . to infuse . . . this part of the natural image of God . . . who has (himself) understanding and will, which will is the same with the Holy Ghost." If then, the beauty that is to appear to the heart's sense is God's own, "Such . . . illumination" must be in a dialectically tight way "the proper work of the Spirit of God."[17] There is nothing recherché about the event: the Spirit lets "spiritual light" into consciousness merely by "discovering the excellency of divine things."[18] God *shines*, and it is the triune role of the Spirit to disclose God in and to our consciousness as he does in and to God himself.

Thus the distinction between God and his saints is preserved, according to Edwards's account, by the trinitarian distinctions themselves. And the difference between natural religion and supernatural illumination is that God the Spirit comes to *play the same role* in saints' consciousness that he does in God's own inner triune life. We might say that in the case of saints, the inner dialectics of created consciousness and the triune dialectics of God as consciousness *mesh* differently than in the case of others.

---

15. Edwards, "Memoirs . . . ," 21.
16. Edwards, *Miscellanies*, 117.
17. Edwards, *Miscellanies*, 732.
18. Edwards, *Miscellanies*, 628.

IV

It should now be apparent on what basis Edwards, himself a person of great reserve, was able to defend the emotionally flooded Awakening. In minute detail, he tried to discriminate between appropriate and inappropriate "affections." But the dominance of affection simply as such was precisely the Awakening's recommendation: "True religion in great part consists in holy affections."[19] Indeed, the "Spirit of God in those that have sound religion" *is* a "temper" of "powerful holy affections."[20] Vice versa, it was exactly the dominance of affection that discredited the revival with its critics. Charles Chauncy's main charge was that the Awakening's manifestations "savoured" of "enthusiasm," that its appeal to the emotions abstracted religion from the control of reasoned choice.[21]

Edwards located the issue with the critics: "In their philosophy, the affections . . . are . . . not appertaining to the noblest part of the soul."[22] It was not only the Awakening's opponents who fit this description. If such proto-"mainline" Protestants as Chauncy viewed the affections as opposed to reason and needing to be overcome by will, such "enthusiastic" revivalists as James Davenport found in them the place of blessed liberation from reason and will alike. To the contrary of both parties, Edwards identified the affections as the very place where reason and will join and where objective divine reality can therefore bind and control consciousness.

In my judgment, here is the *Scheideweg* of American Protestant Christianity. Protestantism's constructive possibility, offered by Edwards, knows the ordering of temporal life as enabled in the heart's prevenient union of knowing and choosing, and knows *that* union constituted in the specific relating of time and eternity which occurs in the triune God's own life. It is the loss of exactly this apprehension that is decisive for the story of American Protestantism.

We must be clear: the place in consciousness to which Edwards assigns affection obtains *only if God is triune.* I acknowledge the hyperbole, but still suggest that the history of American religion has been the actualizing of Edwards's general interpretation of religious experience within an effectively unitarian interpretation of God. Under God so interpreted, the affections can unite consciousness neither with itself nor with God. That religious or other affections

19. Yale Edition, 2:95.
20. Yale Edition, 100.
21. Chauncy, *The Late Religious Commotion in New England Considered* (Boston: T. Fleet, 1743), 9ff.
22. Yale Edition, 4:297.

grasp reality cannot be established from their nature in themselves but only from the role played by the Spirit in God's consciousness and ours. If there is not a decisively trinitarian worship and interpretation of God, religious consciousness, precisely as described by Edwards, must again fall apart into knowledge on the one hand and will on the other. And then the affections must either be identified with will, which itself must then be thought irrational, or they must be assigned to the periphery of consciousness, as "emotions."

The supposition that affections—and especially religious affections—are irrational has continued to determine the shape of American piety and theology. The "liberal" descendents of Charles Chauncy regard religious inclination as intrinsically suspect, in any case to be kept in "the private" sphere and not allowed to contaminate the body politic, where reason must rule. And the many successors of James Davenport have from his day to ours regarded religious inclination, with whatever object or fantasized object it may light upon, as self-justifying and beyond public critique. In practice, the two sects have worked very well together: the first has relegated all religion but Jefferson's to the—for them—irrelevant private sphere, and the second has rejoiced so to be relegated. And it is not only private and public religion that are here divided, but religion and God, insofar as "God" is to be a *name*.

V

Thus far the report and appreciation of Edwards's interpretation of religion. The suggestion it leaves us should be evident: the fatal flaw, which from the Edwardsean *Scheideweg* has led American and Americanized Protestantism on the way it has gone instead of on the way Edwards indicated, is an *inadequately Christian identification of God*. The church, of course, just *is* the community of a specific identification of God; and insofar as that identification becomes imprecise, the church loses all ability appropriately to order its life. But God so identified is also the only candidate for Eternity available to our culture, and insofar as we have lost hold of his specificity, our worldly doings also have become uncontrollable.

Christian identification of God is always reidentification, for folk do not first begin to speak of God when the evangelists arrive. The fruit to date of this enterprise, within the particular history that leads to us, is the doctrine of Trinity. God, say the Christians, is whoever raised Jesus from the dead; the doctrine of Trinity is but the unpacking of this proposition within the terms of Mediterranean antiquity's antecedent interpretation of God. The discourse with which the reidentification is conducted is "christology." Antecedent interpretations seem self-evident: for example, *"Surely* God cannot suffer?" Christological assertions are the gospel's attack on this resistance: "The Invisible is seen . . . , the Ungraspable is laid hold of . . . , the Impassible suffers . . . , the Deathless dies."[23] Christological propositions are right insofar as they compendiously and drastically *offend* any culture's and any generation's self-evidences about God.

Edwards based the cognitive power of sense or "affection," upon which the integrity of religious consciousness depends, on the triunity of religion's true Object. If the suggestion I draw from his analysis is correct, we would expect him to develop a doctrine of Trinity dissenting in some ways from the tradition, and in ways precisely contrary to those that American Protestantism was to take. I conclude my direct reference to Edwards on this point by noting that in the drafts of his unpublished *summa,* just such a doctrine appears. Correlatively, he grasped what he called "Arminianism" *christologically,* as the disintegration of faith into a merely "deistical" knowledge of "God" and a merely sentimental relation to Christ. And, in the drafts, a radical christology appears as well, one citation from which can show its relevance to our matter: God's love, "as it is in the divine nature, is not a passion, is not such love as we feel, but by the Incarnation [God] is really become passionate to his own."[24] Neither do I have space to exploit his christological contribution further.

Of course, Protestantism has had no peculiar doctrines of Trinity or of the person of Christ. I thus acquire the obligation to inquire why shared doctrine has had different consequences for Catholicism and Protestantism. Finally, if indeed the fatal flaw operative in my story is anything so abstract as a defective doctrine of "trinitarian relations" or "hypostatic union," I am obliged to end my essay with some suggestion of the contexts in which practical repair of the defects ought to be undertaken.

VI

First, the Trinity and the Spirit in the Trinity. Ecumenically, faith in Christ is understood to enable and be enabled by the active presence of the Spirit. Ecumenically, the active presence of the Spirit is understood to bring gifts, the last fruition of which will be "salvation." In

---

23. Melito of Sardis, *Antonius Caesar,* 13.
24. Edwards, *Miscellanies,* z.

the Eastern church, the presence and gifts of the Spirit are understood to integrate the believer into the triune Life itself, exactly as Edwards taught. But in the Western church, Edwards's position just at this point is atypical, for it strictly follows from the usual Western doctrine of Trinity that the Spirit cannot play the same role in the consciousness of saints that he plays in the divine Life. Let me say parenthetically that I do not introduce this contrast between Eastern and Western Christianity in order generally to praise the East, but only for historical convenience in making the following few points.

The typical Western position derives from Augustine's attempts to resolve a problem in trinitarian theology: how to distinguish the Spirit's "procession," by which he exists as a divine hypostasis, from his "mission" to the church and to believers' hearts.[25] It would have been better had a resolution not been so vigorously pursued. As it was done, the distinction of that "being breathed" (by which the Spirit is the inner triune bond of Love) from that "being poured out" (by which he is the bond of love between God and believers) became the test case of a general metaphysically ruthless distinction of the "processions" from the "missions": "'mission' and 'sending' . . . are predicated only temporally, 'generation' and 'breathing' only eternally."[26]

It will not be entirely irrelevant to our purpose if I follow the more general point a step or two further. By thus definitionally sorting out what the East had left beneficently confused, Western trinitarianism evacuated its own meaning. For the trinitarian language about the "three hypostases" and their mutually constituting "relations" originally had content as it modeled the plot of salvation's history, in order then to assert this plot as the movement of the divine Life itself; just so, this language is the decisive interpretation of God by the gospel. When the "missions"—that is, the saving history—and the "processions"—that is, the divine Life— are distinguished definitionally by the difference between time and atemporality, the doctrine of Trinity has no purpose.

Augustine himself saw the problem: he explicitly acknowledged that, on his interpretation, when we say "one substance" or "three persons" we communicate nothing more than "one" or "three," using the further verbiage only because it is traditional.[27] It could be but a matter of time before the doctrine of Trinity becomes

---

25. Augustine, *De trinitate*, 5:16 is the classic and indeed foundational instance.
26. Aquinas, *Summa theologiae*, 1.43.2.
27. Augustine, *De trinitate*, 5:10; 7:7-11.

the number mystification Western churchgoers have accepted because they are supposed to, and which they have ignored for all practical religious purposes.

We may ask why Augustine pushed his point, since he understood its consequences. There is no doubt about the answer, as there was not to Augustine. It was his first and last axiom about God, to which all other considerations had to yield: "Speak of the changes of things, and you find 'was' and 'will be'; think God, and you find 'is' where 'was' and 'will be' cannot enter."[28] It is, so far as I can press my understanding of the matter, the great Augustine's remarkably flatfooted and uncritical reception of the Greek interpretation of divine eternity as abstraction *from* time that is the deepest flaw in Western interpretation of God. For if God is God precisely in that there is no "temporal movement of his substance,"[29] language about hypostases constituted in active relations, in "processions," *cannot* be meaningful when used of him.

As we live and think within Western Christianity's way of interpreting God, we cannot know the Spirit's relating us *to* God as his relating us *in* God. For the Spirit's action to set us in relation to the Father and the Son on the one hand and his action to relate the Father and the Son on the other are ontically separate acts. All of which is to say that an Edwardsean grasp of our heart's affection as reality's grasp on us is not available to us—unless we revise our trinitarianism.

But why then does Protestantism seem to need this unavailable insight when Catholicism seems to get along without it? Why, within Protestantism, is the flaw in Western identification of God fatal precisely to belief in God, whereas—I must suppose—it afflicts Catholicism otherwise?

The Augustinian interpretation of God cuts the ground from under that factor in created consciousness which is, precisely according to Augustine, the essential appearance in us of the Spirit's role in God. Our "heart's sense," the aesthetic alteration of consciousness by which the God who is truly Another imposes himself and in the imposing founds the unity of our knowledge of him and our will toward him, cannot fulfill its role over against this God. In Catholicism, something takes its place; in Protestantism, nothing does. And that—within these terms of analysis—is the difference between them.

---

28. Augustine, *In Johannem*, 38:10.
29. Augustine, *De trinitate*, 1:3.

Notoriously, it was debated at the very foundation of Western scholasticism: Can we conceive the *work* of the Spirit in us as identical with his *presence?* It was decided that we cannot. Thereupon, the work of the Spirit was understood as "created grace," as a temporal and *other* love than that by which the Spirit is the bond in God. It is the elaborate understanding and, decisively, *experience* of this grace-given virtue that in Catholicism substitutes for the experience that should belong to Christians. The doctrine of created grace has been a primary target of Protestant polemics from the beginning of the Reformation, and in my judgment rightly, for it puts an experience of "created" qualities—that is, of ourselves—where there should be experience of the Father and the Son in the Spirit. But it cannot be said that those polemics have done more than create a vacuum; polemics alone can hardly foster enjoyment of God. Catholicism has sustained a—lamentably—causal relation of the soul's life to God; Protestantism must either recover a true trinitarianism or lose the relation to God altogether.

VII

Standard Western theology has cultivated a precise christological correlate to its enfeebled trinitarianism. The christological refraction of our "flaw" will perhaps most clearly display its relevance to Protestantism's current dissociation of time from eternity, since Christ *is*, of course, the relation of time to eternity as the gospel proclaims it. My thesis in this context is that, having made the *Tome* of Leo its christological text, Western Christianity *must* be either sacramentalist or sacramentarian, turned in on its ecclesial self or unbelieving. Catholicism and Protestantism, each with its besetting errors, are condemned by their shared christology to circle each other in mutual attraction and condemnation, so long as the christology is not fixed.

Christology Eastern and Western can begin for our purposes at Chalcedon. It is regularly said to be Chalcedon's virtue that it only set boundaries. By the same token, its formulas can be read in very different ways. There are in Christ, it is said, "humanity" and "deity," two "natures" intact, united as and only as "one hypostasis." But what do these rules *say?*

Key interpretive phrases of Chalcedon's decrees were present at Western insistence, demanded by the famous *Tome* of Pope Leo; and it is these phrases and the *Tome* itself, authorized by attachment to Chalcedon's decrees as allowed interpretation, that have in fact been the functioning *Western* dogma. I cite the *Tome's* key passage, in somewhat disrespectfully modern translation: "Each nature does its own thing, in cooperation with the other."[30] (I had almost translated ". . . so long as it doesn't hurt the other.")

Western scholasticism conducted a brilliant analytical development of Leonine christology: here, as often, analytical ingenuity was provoked exactly by paucity of matter. It is caricature to describe "*the* scholastic christology," but I must allow myself the caricature. The foundation is so cleaving a distinction between a "hypostasis" and the "nature(s)" of which it is the hypostasis that from the unity of plural natures in one hypostasis nothing at all immediately follows for the unified natures. The fundamental Chalcedonian assertion, that God the Logos and humanity are "one hypostasis," is by this analysis a purely—in our terms—logical assertion: that *somehow or other* propositions are true that attribute acts or characteristics of either "nature" to one final subject of predication.[31] Thus the whole matter of "The Logos is this man" comes to be stated by analysis of such predications, by the doctrine of "communication of attributes."

When we then examine the scholastic version of the doctrine of communication of attributes, we find again that Leo is perfectly obeyed. The grammatical subjects of such propositions as "Jesus will judge the quick and the dead" or "The Logos was born of Mary" are said to be only alternative ways of denoting the same real subject, the one hypostasis *in* its distinction from the nature(s) it hypostasizes; about God the Logos or the man Jesus they say nothing whatever directly. And even read so, they are to be classified as assertions *in verbo* not *in re*[32]—that is, although they are *true* as they stand, they do not as they stand represent the form of the fact they state. To obtain from, for example, the proposition "The Logos was

---

30. Leo of Rome, *Letter to Flavian of Antioch* (COD: 77-82): "Agit enim utraque forma cum alterius communione quod proprium est."

31. So, for example, Duns Scotus: the Logos is a merely "relative" hypostasis and so has, *as* the Logos, no efficacy. Thus, since it is the Logos as hypostatically distinct that is incarnate, the Logos's union with a human nature has no effect thereon. Nor is the Logos affected by the union, since as God he cannot in any case be affected. That the Logos as hypostasis is the hypostasis of the human nature thus means only that it is the "*suppositum*" of that nature, that which is denoted by the subject of propositions asserting the nature's characteristics of something. See, for example, "*The Oxford Manuscript*," III, 1.

32. For example in this case, see Bonaventura, *Four Books of Sentences*, 3; 14.3.3; 21.2.3; 22.1.2. A sample: "unde filius Dei dicitur fuisse mortuus, quia fuit homo, in quo fuit passio mortis," 21.2.3.

born of Mary" a proposition that reflects the fact that verifies it, it must be translated into "The man Jesus (who is hypostatically one with the Logos) was born of Mary."

There is plainly here a circle that will eventually evacuate meaning. On the one hand, that the Logos and Jesus are one hypostasis is taken as sheer permission to assert propositions that "communicate attributes." On the other hand, such propositions are said to be true only by way of a detour through the hypostatic union. My concern here is not with the theoretical problem as such, nor with the means the scholastics used to deal with it.[33] The point for present purposes is that this christology leaves God as such—the divine "nature"—utterly uninterpreted by what happens with Jesus. Which is to say, it evades the purpose of christology.

Perhaps we may translate these abstractions into the churchly reality they reflect and support by instancing a classic controversy between Catholicism and Protestantism. From its beginning, the Western church has been upset by controversy over Christ's presence in the Supper—such as has never afflicted the East. The question, of course, is real: How *does* the risen Christ come to be embodied as loaf and cup?

Western reflection has typically worried about this question within strict metaphysical parameters. A *body*, it is presupposed, must have its own place, distinct from all other places. That given, we know where Christ's body is: at the right hand of the Father in heaven. And it will hardly do to think that Christ *travels* from heaven to all those separated appointments.[34] Thus the position is: the body of Christ must be "in the sacrament . . . in a special way unique to the sacrament."[35]

Therewith, however, the question of *truth* becomes acute. And no *christological* answer can be given so long as we are faithful to Leo, for he allows no participation by Christ's bodily humanity in God's transcendence of space and time. Christ's presence as loaf and cup must therefore be a supernatural event *additional* to those of Incarnation and Resurrection.[36] But the faithful can hardly be left to wonder at each Supper whether the miracle is this time happening; the supernatural act must be *reliable*. The Catholic solution has been that God grants to the church, in its own sacramental structure, the

---

33. These turn out to exploit the doctrine of "created graces" again! See Bonaventura, *Four Books of Sentences*, 3; 14.1.1-2.

34. See, for example, Aquinas, *Summa theologiae*, 3.75.2.

35. Aquinas, *Summa theologiae*, 3.75.1 ad 3.

36. See Aquinas, *Summa theologiae*, 3.75.4.

authority to invoke the supernatural event, to say "This is my body" and know that it is true because the church says it.

What then if we "protest" such churchly authority? It depends on the grounds of the protest. It could be protested that the Catholic development gives to *ecclesiology* a role that belongs to *christology*. (If I may insert one word for my own ecclesial tradition, this was the specifically Lutheran protest.) By and large, however, Protestantism has instead assigned to *anthropology* the very same role that Catholicism assigned to ecclesiology. Protestantism assigns to the individual's faith the authority that Catholicism assigns to the church's faith.[37] The difference, of course, is that the individual cannot resolve the unity of his or her knowing and willing, since the individual is the problem—unless we are willing, as German idealism was, to identify conscious individuality and deity.

And so finally to come to the point: this christology leaves our relation to God in the very situation from which Edwards thought the Incarnation was to rescue us. Let me cite the rest of the passage from Edwards with which I introduced the subject of christology: "by the Incarnation [God the Logos] is really become passionate to his own, so that he loves them with such a sort of love as we have . . . to those we most dearly love. . . . So that now when we delight ourselves at the thought of God loving us, we need not have that allay of our pleasure . . . that though he loved us yet we could not conceive of that love."[38]

Picking up my remaining assignment, I would note that within Catholicism our relation to God can be sundered into an intellectualism so extreme that one can say "I believe whatever the church teaches" and maintain a "Mary-Joseph-Jesus" piety of a sentimentality that Protestantism cannot match. Yet the two never quite fall apart to destroy the relation to God altogether, since the same *institution* sponsors and guarantees both. Take from the church its capacity to guarantee and sponsor such matters, leaving the sundering otherwise undealt with, and Protestant unbelief is inevitable.

VIII

I turn finally to the chief matter at hand: What practically is to be done about these things? Let me this time start with christological points.

---

37. See, for example, the doctrine of Theodore Beza, as finely reported by Jill Raitt in *The Eucharistic Theology of Theodore Beza* (Chambersburg: AAR, 1972).

38. Jonathan Edwards, *Miscellanies*, z.

It will, for a first negative point, only make matters worse to exhort our fellow believers to turn from their preoccupation with temporal orderings to concern for the eternal. That they have been taught to think of the eternal as what they must *turn to* from time is the cause of our problem. The fashionable talk about the "worldliness" and "temporality" of the gospel does, after all, have biblical reason. Nor, if Peter Berger is rightly unwilling to leave theology to the theologians, have I much confidence that the quality of discourse about *worldly* matters will be greatly improved by interdicting it in the pulpit and leaving it to the various worldly "experts." What ails our fashionable theologies is not that they find the eternal in time but that they find it in temporalities generally rather than in the specific temporality named Jesus. And *that*, I suggest, is the fault of a traditional christology which, while whetting a taste for "incarnational principles" and the like, leaves us without the real Incarnation.

What we have instead to do is to offend as mightily as we can the notion of Eternity that makes him seem both abstracted from time and less interesting than time. God, the church must again learn to say, is everything we have not supposed he is, in that the narrative about Jesus is the narrative about him. Probably, the christological tradition has been so broken off within Protestantism that there can be little point in amending its technicalities. Rather, we should speak directly within christology's original functional context: the critique of religion by what is true of the Crucified and Risen Man.

Is it thought in Protestantism that "of course" God is not "to blame" when bad things happen to good people? Let someone say, "But only consider what the Father did to the Son!" Is it self-evident that "the Christ" must be of neuter gender? Or of one's own or no ethnicity? Let someone point out that Jesus' mission was so profoundly subversive that it offended all hands equally, the zealots as deeply as the Sadducees. Let us with Luther insist against Erasmus that it is precisely God's free and—by us—unpredictable *grace* that is sovereign and that this grace must be honored though all order fall, whether on earth or in heaven.

Ironically, precisely as we thus *offend* the self-evidences about God, "affection" becomes possible between him and us. Interpreting Eternity by Jesus, we do not make Eternity "human" in James Turner's use of the word, but we do make him human in the sense of the Scriptures. We do not make God *gemütlich*, but we do make him passionate, one to whom we can be bound in affection and who can be known in the quality of the affection granted. The offense of God-interpreted-by-Jesus is the offense of unmitigated and unstoppable affection. And, in further irony, it is precisely as we *thus* find God in time that we will gain the distance from temporal affairs that is, as Peter Berger insists, the condition of our ability to order them.

Let me append one word on the christological technicalities for those interested in such matters. In the doctrine proposed, it will be impossible to speak even metaphysically about a "hypostasis" in abstraction from the "nature(s)" of which it is the hypostasis. The "communication of attributes" will therefore be understood as *in re* and not merely *in verbo* and will, moreover, include not only the eccentric Lutheran *genus maiestaticum* but the always feared *genus tapeinoticum:* Jesus the man will be identified as God, and God the Son will be understood to be *as* God the subject of the narrative by which the human life of Jesus is identified. That is to say that the big theological "omni"-words will be seen to hold of the human Jesus because they are defined by his story. What, for example, does it mean that God is—"of course"—"omnipresent"? An adequate christological discourse will allow the word to be defined by neither antique nor modern culture religion; it will mean neither that God is distant and ungraspable nor that God is always "with us," as on our side; we will use the word to say with Johannes Brenz that all creation is but one place before God's intention, the place picked out by the cross.[39]

IX

And so in conclusion, the Trinity. My technical proposal can come at the beginning, since it but extends the christological proposal. If Jesus is *in fact* the Logos as just insisted, then *he*, and not a separately describable "Logos," is the "second hypostasis" in God. Then very directly the history enacted between him and the Transcendence he addressed as "Father" and the Spirit of their converse *is* God. And then, again very directly, as we are addressed in this converse and brought into it in the church, the Spirit plays the same role in our lives that he does in God. The systematicians will tell me of the problems posed by such assertions, and perhaps I know of them; they are not my present concern.

Where can renewed trinitarianism be cultivated? In the home and functional context of trinitarianism: the liturgy. The triune name and the dialectics of trinitarian description are the gospel's *identification* of God, and it is in hearing from God and calling upon him that

---

39. See, for example, Johannes Brenz, *De personalis unione duarum naturarum in Christo* (Tübingen: n.p., 1561).

we need to identify him. It is not that the one and only God cannot intercept prayers however addressed, but that is his concern. Ours is to make use of the great gift of the gospel: not to pray at random, but to address a specified God whose intention and character are known to us. From the very first, the home of the triune name and of all trinitarian identification of God was the liturgy. It may be thought that trinitarian renewal is *always* liturgical renewal, but at least among Protestants and under the brokenness of the doctrinal tradition, no other possibility is anyway now open.

With what prayer are the bread and cup brought before God and the people? With the ancient praise of the Father for remembrance of the Son and under evocation of the Spirit? Or with no prayer at all, as commonly among the Methodists? Or with a "christomonistic" prayer, as commonly among Lutherans? Or with the old Roman canon and its imitators, in which only the most recondite scholarship can recognize the triune structure? Let us, if we wish to repair Protestantism's ability to order its times by ordering them to God, attend to just such matters.

With what name do we baptize or bless? With, perhaps, an inclusive expression as "Parent, Child, and Spirit" or to the same purpose in such context, "Creator, Redeemer, and Sanctifier"? If we are concerned for Protestantism's fidelity to the one and only God, it will be vital testimony to rise and leave the place of such parody. With what words do we comfort the suffering? With reference to "God's" good will? If we are concerned for the order of time and eternity, let it be instead with "In the name of God, Father, Son, and Spirit, I . . ."

I will break off the rhetorical questions. A "constructive Protestant response to Christian unbelief" will consist in two reforms. We will overcome the heritage of the Western church's feeble trinitarianism by trinitarian reform of worship; and we will overcome the correlated heritage of the Western church's feeble christology by christological critique of religion. Jonathan Edwards, be it noted, saw both necessities. American Protestantism missed the opportunity he offered. *If* there is still opportunity, there cannot be many to come. For while Catholic error can be reformed, Protestant unbelief can only be evangelized from outside.

Only if Protestantism learns again to love God with the intellect and know him with the will, only if it can recover the integrity of religious affection will it be able to survive its abjuration of the church that administers grace. To do that, it must radicalize in unheard-of ways the central Christian dogmas. And it must in this attempt start from near scratch.

Fortunately, the places of such starting—the liturgy and critique —will be *good* places to be. For there is one last strand to be taken up. Christological critique consists in uncovering the *truth* of God and trinitarian dialectics in *displaying* it. But the *splendor veritatis* is *beauty;* we are back with Edwards. I will conclude with a story I read as a very young theologian and have never forgotten, though I have forgotten its attribution.

A visionary monk in his dream was taken on one of those tours of heaven and its notables that were once so popular. Gorged with splendors and saints, he was suddenly dashed by realization of an appalling absence. "Where," he cried, "is Augustine?" "Oh," said his angel guide, "he is higher yet, before the very Trinity, *speculating* thereon through all eternity."

The Story of an Encounter

Paul T. Stallsworth

Nature seemed to be resisting—or at least attempting to disorder—the conference, which was titled "The Ordering of Our Life, Temporal and Eternal." New York City's heaviest snow in four years had fallen on 22 January 1987, the day before the conference was to begin. The snow that day, as well as minor fires on several subway lines, had severely limited attendance at the third annual Erasmus Lecture at Saint Peter's Lutheran Church at Citicorp Center. But as it turned out, nature was not unmercifully cruel to this enterprise, for the lecture by Peter L. Berger indeed took place, as did the two-day conference.

The Princeton Club of New York provided the space and, thankfully, the heat for the conference. In addition, four presenters provided papers for the conference. Twenty participants—from colleges, universities, seminaries, and publication offices—provided plenty of comment on the conference papers. And, Pastor Richard John Neuhaus, the director of the Rockford Institute Center on Religion & Society and the moderator of the two-day conversation, provided the introduction for the conference. He started things off this way: "Some months ago the observation was made that there is today as severe an eclipse of the gospel as was the case in the sixteenth century. That observation may be true or false. If it is true, there would seem to be an urgent need for something like a reformation. Obviously, it would cut across all of the ecclesial and denominational lines which came out of the sixteenth-century Reformation. Like the sixteenth-century Reformation, it would be contending for the gospel. The assumption of this conference is that at the heart of today's eclipse of the gospel is a deeper eclipse of belief in God. We are talking about unbelief."

Then Neuhaus sketched the general flow of the conference conversation as he envisioned it. Peter Berger's paper, which had served as the Erasmus Lecture the evening prior, would set up the sociological framework for the discussion of apostasy in American Protestantism. Berger would be followed by James Turner, who would give a historical overview of religious leadership in America trying to cope with modernity. A theological duo (as opposed to duel) would complete the conference. Roman Catholic Avery Dulles would refer to and seek to go beyond the Hartford Appeal, which was completed in January of 1975, and its perspective on the church in the modern world. Lutheran Robert Jenson would contend that the possibility of reformation hinges largely on the church's operating idea of God.

APOSTASY AND SOCIOLOGY

To launch into the discussion of his paper, Peter Berger, a University Professor at Boston University, asked a question framed by anti–Vietnam War rhetoric and laced with humor: "What would happen if we declared a reformation and nobody came?"

But then he started talking sociology, and when Berger talks sociology he tends to get serious. He nicely and neatly summarized the argument of his paper: "My basic sociological proposition is that the whole drama of belief and unbelief, faith and secularization, in the contemporary American situation is embedded in a cultural conflict and that this cultural conflict is embedded in a class conflict. In the paper I am doing three things. First, I identify two major parties in this conflict. Let us call them in shorthand terms the Right and the Left. Sociologically speaking I make no judgments about them at all. All I try to do is understand what is going on among them. Let me put it this way. Sociologically this is a nonjudgmental operation; I do not judge either party. Second, I make a very emphatic moral judgment. To my mind, on the major issues that divide these two camps, there is no moral equivalence. It seems to me that the Left's positions, which have become established in a substantial segment of American religion, are morally reprehensible. I make a moral argument on that. Third, theologically I judge both parties. Both the Right and the Left, when they push their agendas into the center of the life of the church, are equally guilty of apostasy."

Thomas Oden, who teaches theology at Drew University, remained skeptical of Berger's sociological analysis. He thought Berger's New Class/Old Class scheme a bit of an oversimplification. After all, Oden said, the socio-economic location of several individuals sitting around the conference table would suggest that they ought to be card-carrying members of the New Class, and yet they are not. Oden restated his point by noting that "There are not just two types of bumper stickers in America today—New Class and Old Class." The middle class is splintered into *many* camps, he insisted, not just two.

Oden then challenged the sociological enterprise to take a lesson from theology. "Max Weber could have tried to explain to John Wesley why the poor became rich. His explanation, of course, would be that we have class mobility and that that is a predictor of political ideology and economic productivity. It seems to me that Wesley had another explanation for why the poor were becoming rich, why his own poor in his own societies were becoming rich. It had to do with the desperate wickedness of the heart, it had to do with original sin, it had to do with the proneness of the heart toward acquisition, and it had to do with idolatry. I wonder if Weber could have learned from Wesley as well as if Wesley might have learned from Weber about these alternative explanations of acquisition."

Not one to let such challenges go by the wayside, Berger answered Oden. "Are some of us sitting around this table an argument against the New Class thesis? No, not at all. All social-scientific statements are statements of a frequency distribution. Take for example, in the 1950s, one of the great, intellectually stunning statistical studies, the Kinsey Report. It made the statement that working-class people tend to make love in the dark while middle-class people leave the lights on. That is a statistical statement. Of course there were thousands of working-class people who made love under floodlights and middle-class people who crept under the blankets and put blindfolds on. Again, it is a statistical statement. In other words, if I see an individual and know nothing about that individual except his income and education, can I predict his sexual habits or his political opinions with a certain degree of *probability*? The answer is Yes, I can. In the New Class thesis we are beginning to have an increasing body of supporting data.

"In terms of religion," Berger continued, "let me refer to the very interesting survey made by the Roper Center on behalf of *This World* magazine. That survey has very hard data on the New Class thesis. Still, there are always traitors to their class."

Oden was not altogether convinced. "Isn't it ironic that all of those statistics, which I can certainly affirm and in which the frequency distribution is evident, could not have predicted a Peter Berger?"

To which the allegedly unpredictable Berger responded, "No statistical data can ever predict an individual case. What's ironic about it?"

"I am enjoying the irony," said Oden. "You are rejecting it on scientific grounds. I'll just continue to enjoy it." Several of the conferees seemed to be enjoying the Berger-Oden exchange, if the chuckles around the table were any indication.

But Berger got the last word with Oden: "I'll enjoy it with you in the sense that there is an unpredictability and spontaneity about human beings."

Shifting the gears of the discussion, Fr. Avery Dulles, a Catholic University professor of theology, wondered aloud about the ideology and interests of the New Class. "Why does the new knowledge class want to deemphasize military power and to expand the welfare state? Why is it in this class's interests to do that? It might very well have interests in the opposite direction."

Berger was ready and waiting with a reply. "Why is the New Class inclined in the direction of the expansion of the welfare state? Because it is in its interests to be so inclined. The new middle class, compared to the old middle class, is much more heavily dependent on government funding. Therefore, it has a vested interest in the expansion of government. The New Class is heavily into the redistribution mechanism of the modern welfare state. It has a vested interest in redistribution rather than production." He went on to say that "the New Class makes its livelihood out of the production and distribution of symbolic knowledge. By symbolic knowledge I mean knowledge which is not directly related to material production and material services." It might be noted that while symbolic knowledge has a certain role to play in the maintenance of military power, that role is rather minor when compared with the major role that symbolic knowledge plays in the area of government-provided human services.

Is It Really Apostasy?

David Lotz, a historian at Union Theological Seminary in New York, readily admitted that the church has a problem today. But he had a problem with calling that problem *apostasy*. "Berger defines *apostasy* as the substitution of another gospel for the gospel of Jesus Christ. So are we talking about apostasy, or are we speaking of the muting of the gospel, or confusion about what the gospel is, or confusion about law and gospel?

"After twenty-three years in theological education in one of the leading liberal seminaries and after involvement with faculty and with several thousand students, I see today's fundamental problem as moralism. By this I mean moral imperatives that are increasingly phrased in the language of political policy. The basic problem is that these moral imperatives are set forth without any endeavor to link them to the dynamics of the gospel. If that were done more carefully and thoughtfully, it might be seen that the gospel is being muted or distorted.

"As a historian of the church, I am most reluctant to operate with an apostasy model. If you want to invoke the Reformation, we would not conclude, as historians, that in the Reformation we are dealing with apostasy. Confusion of law and gospel, yes. But I do not read the Book of Concord, and above all the Augsburg Confession, as operating under an apostasy mode. Or one can look at Luther's Treatise of 1528 concerning the Anabaptists, in which there is an explicit acknowledgment of what has been owed to the Roman Church and that the gospel is indeed still preached within that church."

Berger proceeded to offer a defense of his use of the word *apostasy*. "You want me to de-escalate the language," Berger conjectured. "Apostasy is terrible, so why don't I say 'muting of the gospel' or 'confusion'? Sure. I understand your point. But I think I will stick to the stronger language. I take it for granted that within this 'massive perdition,' in which I see especially mainline Protestantism in the Western world, there are faithful people. There are places where the gospel is being preached and the sacraments are being administered faithfully to people who suffer and die in the Christian faith. All that is well and good. That always happens, and it is always a consolation. However, if one looks at the degree of aggressive and militantly stupid dogmatism which permeates the contemporary life of the church in Western countries, one finds that it is not just here and there; it is all over the place. You can very rarely enter a church building for a service without all of this stuff being thrown at you. Is this simply a muting? I think it is something stronger than that. In today's massive confusion, the stronger term, *apostasy*, is appropriate."

Lotz followed, "This is of great concern to me, because our diagnosis of the malady will shape our recommendations for the treatment."

Berger would not budge. "You are arguing about the language. That is not so unimportant. For me, this situation stinks. There is a stench about it for me. It involves a corruption, a diversion of the church from its proper task. What kind of language do you use when you face that? If we decide not to use *apostasy*, we will still have to use extremely strong language, because we are dealing with an extremely perverse situation."

The next speaker, Richard Neuhaus, came to Berger's defense

on the apostasy issue, arguing that "the critical point for Augustine and Luther is whether neighbor love—including neighbor love in the political arena—is salvific or not. Is it true that today, pervasively in the church, programs of sociopolitical change and other forms of service to the neighbor are presented as programs of salvation? I think the answer is Yes. Cardinal Ratzinger, the 1988 Erasmus Lecturer, in the Instruction on Christian Freedom and Liberation draws the line at exactly that point, in good Augustinian-Lutheran fashion. He says this is the heresy. Indeed, he calls it not apostasy but an abandonment of the gospel."

Neuhaus continued his defense: "Berger is saying that the situation today in the church is comparable to the situation of the Christians in Galatia. Was Saint Paul justified in saying 'Let them be accursed'? Obviously, he thought the true gospel had been displaced by another gospel, and he said that those who preach this other gospel are to be accursed. In what informed sort of way are we prepared to say that there are some analogies that need to be candidly and straightforwardly pressed?"

Berger lightened things up by joking that he now understood the grand design of the Erasmus Lectures: "In 1987 you get the Little Inquisitor, in 1988 you get the Grand Inquisitor." For once everybody agreed in laughter.

Then Berger commented on the business of cursing. He began with a confession: "I'm a liberal Protestant. I don't know who has the authority to curse. Paul obviously thought he had it. I know I don't have it. But let me repeat a point I made in the lecture. There is a *built-in* curse to all of this. There is no need for apostles, or popes, or councils of churches to say 'anathema sit.' The built-inness is the bondage to history. To me the irony is that especially people who are politically active know how awful this whole thing is if what you do turns out to be the opposite. You do something good and after a little while it turns out to be evil. You cannot act politically without making decisions which involve the suffering and death of other people and your own guilt."

The fourth conference presenter, Dr. Robert Jenson, who taught at the Lutheran Theological Seminary in Gettysburg and now teaches at St. Olaf College, joined Berger and Neuhaus in favoring apostasy language. "I have a suggestion about this word *apostasy*. I think I have to defend its use because in some moments of journalistic frenzy I have used it too. But seriously, the argument that goes on in the church (which is shorthand for what we can call *theology*) about what ought the church to be doing and saying and supporting has always been done badly. Sometimes it is done so badly that one has to refer to it as heresy. It seems to me that one could refer to it as apostasy when the argument is met with the question 'Who cares?' inside the church. At least within my little part of the church that regularly happens."

Allan Carlson, president of the Rockford Institute, specified the forms that modern apostasy seems to be taking. "The first is Marxism, the march of Marxism in its various forms through the institutions and through the world of the intellect. That includes the materialistic interpretation of history and the use of class conflict as the engine of change. Peter Berger sees that, in various forms, as subverting the gospel in a very fundamental way. Another movement that represents a similar fundamental threat is feminism. Inclusive language is a manifestation of this other political-social movement that has been gaining ground for over two hundred years. Both Marxism and feminism have ways of transforming what has been Christian orthodoxy into another vehicle of class oppression or patriarchal oppression."

Carlson's comment apparently struck home. Berger responded, "I'm bugged more by moral than theological issues. The feminists, on the whole, bother me less. They have done some good, but they have done a lot of harm. It's Marxism that bothers me much more. The issue here again is how one sees the possibilities of mitigating the misery and tyranny by which the world is plagued. Marxism and all socialist ideologies have a fundamentally flawed perception about what to do about poverty. Therefore they help to perpetuate poverty, which is tragic in a country like the United States and apocalyptically tragic in countries where people actually starve to death. Also, Marxism has been—at least since the demise of Fascism—the single major legitimation of tyranny in the world."

A predictable but nonetheless important point was raised by Werner Dannhauser, a Cornell professor who was teaching for a year at the University of Chicago. "We ought to be suspicious because among some of us this notion of apostasy coincided with our fear that religion was going to the left. We did not, with equal fervor, resent the linkage of religion to patriotism and the things of the right. The origins of our concern are suspicious."

Once again, Neuhaus: "When Christianity in America was closely associated with the almost absolute legitimation of 'the American way of life,' Peter Berger was writing *The Noise of Solemn Assemblies*, which is very much in the Will Herberg camp of calling that apostasy, although the word was not used. Wouldn't that be true of most of us?"

Berger's self-defense followed. Whether one sees apostasy on the right or on the left "has to do with where one lives. I live in Boston. If I lived in Dallas, I might be more motivated to worry about the New Right. In Boston you can hardly find evidence of it. Still, the transpolitical character of the Christian faith hits in all directions."

Those who tend to replace religious belief with politics understandably fail to see their own mistake, commented Brian Benestad, a University of Scranton professor. "For example, the Roman Catholic bishops do not even recognize that they are stating their political opinions in their recent pastorals." This was recently revealed in an incident that Benestad recounted. In the presence of several bishops it was claimed that the pastoral on the economy leaned to the left. When a Catholic bishop disagreed, "He got up and said that this claim was wrong and that the letter was simply echoing gospel values."

Fr. Dulles expressed a similar concern: "On this faith-and-justice business, it is curious how faith and justice always means justice. Nobody ever discusses anything about faith."

At least one Roman Catholic among the conferees, Margaret Steinfels of *Commonweal,* was puzzled by this talk of a leftish gospel. She spoke out of experience and from history. "Most of the gospel talk in Roman Catholicism that is heard by Roman Catholics is in the Sunday sermons. As an habitué of the liturgy, I am puzzled by this characterizing it as left of center. In the Archdiocese of New York— and I would bet in Boston and Chicago and various other places— the sermon is not political at all. It connects with the lectionary readings of the day. I cannot remember the last politically left-of-center sermon I heard inside a Catholic church. Perhaps the political phenomenon we are discussing is restricted to university campuses.

"My images of the Catholic Church in politics include the Austrian bishops welcoming the Nazis, and the Spanish bishops blessing Franco, and more recently Cardinal Cooke sitting in a fighter plane in Vietnam. The Catholic Church has always been political, it has always blessed politics, and it always tended to bless politics that are divergent from the gospel and that are on the right, not the left."

This roused Berger to disagree: "The two major Roman Catholic statements on political issues in recent years have been the letters on the economy and on war and peace. There is no way you can read them and not say they are left of center. Empirically, the views presented in both letters are highly consonant with the views that dominate the left wing of the Democratic Party."

To which Steinfels took exception by saying, "I am hard-pressed to find the economics pastoral too left of anything. It depends where

one locates the nuclear question to know how left of center that is."
The relativism implied by Steinfels's second point could easily be
extended to suggest the obvious: what one deems as politically left
and right depends in large part on where one is seated at the table of
politics.

On the issue of apostasy language the conference was divided.
Some thought "apostasy" accurately describes the current state of
many American churches. Others, notably several of the Roman
Catholics present, thought the term to be excessive. But this lack of
consensus did not impede the discussion of other issues.

Metapolitics

Ernest Fortin of Boston College was the first to use a word that
would quickly become a point of reference in the discussion—
metapolitical. "Berger means that Christianity is metapolitical, in the
strict sense. Christianity is not just a transnational religion. It rises
above the level of political life. It opens up a new dimension that
cannot be found in political life as such, and it somehow comple-
ments that political life."

Fortin then probed the implications of metapolitical Christianity. "The question then becomes how Christianity relates itself to
the world. It is all right to say that Christianity is transpolitical or
metapolitical, that it does not advocate any particular form of
government or regime or constitutional arrangement. But still,
Christianity does call us to be of service to other human beings. That
means that one cannot be indifferent to the political order, even if
one has something that transcends it." That leads the church to ask
how it should function within society. Unfortunately, said Fortin,
"that is the kind of question that cannot be answered a priori. You
can't indicate in advance what the appropriate solution in a particular society should be, because it depends to a very large extent
on considerations that cannot be known in advance."

Dannhauser picked up on Fortin's concerns about the church in
the world and sharpened the idea of metapolitics. "The metapolitical view of religion leads to a kind of bracketing of the two realms.
It is certainly true that God is neither a Republican nor a Democrat.
But it must be true, somehow, that religion—and Christianity in
particular—has more affinity with certain kinds of regimes than
with other kinds of regimes."

Always, or at least oftentimes, the skeptic, Robert Jenson questioned the metapolitical character of Christianity. First he admitted
that "I do have some problem with calling Christianity metapoliti-

cal. Doubtless, there is something right about that. But on the other hand, Peter Berger, who points to the metapolitical character of Christianity, is not afraid to make moral judgments about politics. What he then does is constantly and clearly distinguish those from theological judgments. I doubt, even though I am a Lutheran, that that distinction can be made quite that bluntly."

Then the St. Olaf theologian speculated on reasons behind and results of Berger's style of metapolitics. "If we say, as Berger seems to say, that the gospel is really, always, and only forgiveness and the permission to try again next time but that it doesn't have any moral content of its own, then correlated with that is a particular kind of use of Augustine's model—love God and do as you please. That is, love God for being so generous and merciful, and then generate your own ethics from what seems good to you. That particular use of the justification doctrine together with a particular kind of situation ethic has been the framework for political action in many churches—including my own Lutheran church. Why, for example, does the homosexuality document just issued by my own church amount to an explicit declaration that the one thing the church does not want to do is quote the Bible, or Augustine, or Luther on the issue? Instead, it takes a poll about how the church feels about the issue these days. They can justify that out of a certain doctrine of justification. That is why I worry about Peter Berger's use of this particular doctrine of justification as his way of separating theological judgment and moral judgment."

Let's be realistic, interjected Dannhauser. "Is the church going to be metapolitical about slavery in this day and age? After all, slavery is a political institution."

After patiently listening to the several critiques of his so-called metapolitical view of Christianity, it was Berger's turn to speak. "Whether one has this or that doctrine of justification or sanctification or of the uses of the law, the relation between the theological position and concrete moral choices in the political arena is an indirect one. I don't think there is a way to deduce concrete political choices in a direct and unambiguous way from notions of the political uses of the law or the sanctification of creation. There is one important distinction here. I have no doubt that from a Christian or Jewish point of view slavery must be condemned. Slavery is an unambiguous violation of human dignity with respect to the God of creation. But it is very different to ask what one does politically to change slavery."

Berger proceeded to support his thesis with two concrete examples. First, "If one talks about slavery today, the most relevant political reality is totalitarianism. Full-blown totalitarian societies are slave societies. What else does one call a person who works for somebody else, who cannot enjoy the fruits of his own labor, and who cannot even leave his place of employment without the permission of the employer? That is slavery. Totalitarianism, in all its forms, should be absolutely condemned as a violation of God's will for human beings. But what political agenda follows from this? If I lived in Eastern Europe, I think I would be rather conservative about what I could do about that situation. Trying to abolish totalitarianism at the risk of nuclear war is not an agenda I would wish to follow. Armed resistance against Soviet power in Eastern Europe is a hopeless enterprise. So what does one do? I don't know. The absolute condemnation of totalitarianism does not in an easy way lead to a course of action for a Christian in Poland or the Soviet Union or China.

"Second, take slavery in the historically precise sense—say, slavery in the United States in the nineteenth century. Let us put ourselves mentally, with our present moral judgment and sensibilities, in the year 1850. What would we have said about slavery in the South? I hope we would have condemned it, though I am well aware that many Christians in the South and elsewhere did not condemn it. Would we have wanted to abolish it at the risk of the Civil War, in which one million people were killed? Perhaps we would have looked for ways to get rid of slavery other than the unspeakable bloodbath that in the end abolished it. Maybe we would have concluded it worth the price. But it is not an easy step from the condemnation of slavery to 'The Battle Hymn of the Republic.'"

On that point, as on few others, there was a certain consensus.

Ecclesiology at Issue

The character and mission of the church soon moved to the center of the conference conversation. In his paper Peter Berger had raised the issue of the church. Several others were now ready to raise the issue again.

Berger's view of the church, contended Oden, is too nonexemplary and deconstructionist. That is to say, Oden did not like Berger's perspective on the church. "Peter Berger says that no Christian group has ever lived up to the promise of Galatians 3:28," said Oden. "Does he mean—not the New Testament church, not the church at Antioch, not the church at Rome, not the early Franciscans, not Wesley's societies? Does he really mean that we have no examples of this? It seems to me that in fact we do have some remarkable examples, particularly of the church under conditions of persecution, of radical accountability under the promise of Galatians 3:28, a radical sense of living in Christ which transcends the social divisions and inequities that pervade human existence.

"You say the gospel liberates by relativizing all worldly realities. That seems to be a negative way of talking about something that could be put positively as faith in God's transcending grace and power and providence, that works in and through and beyond these relativizations. Do we want to get trapped into accepting that what the church finally has to offer the world is a notion of the relativization of value? It seems to me that the church has something more than that to offer."

If Berger's idea of the church seemed to lack a constructive element, so did his idea of salvation, in the eyes of the assistant director of the Rockford Institute Center on Religion & Society, Paul Stallsworth. "In Berger's paper, justification by faith comes out again and again as *the* gospel. However, according to the Wesleyan tradition, this omits a very important aspect of the gospel, of salvation, and that is the sanctificationist emphasis. We must be clear about sanctification being a part of the gospel and salvation. Sanctification involves not just what God does *for us*, but also what God does *in us*. It has to do with God moving us toward perfection, or toward improvement. This of course involves neighbor love, our action in the world, our vocations."

Ken Myers, formerly editor of *This World*, joined in regarding the justification/sanctification problem. "Justification and sanctification are two distinct but organically related actions of God, with distinct human responsibilities and activities. Perhaps the root of apostasy is to confuse or deny any distinction between justification and sanctification. When those two aspects of salvation are confused, is the transcendence of the righteousness of God effectively denied?"

Stallsworth then tied together, or attempted to tie together, various points on sanctification, apostasy, and the churches today: "In the last chapter of Galatians Paul writes, 'Neither circumcision nor uncircumcision mean anything. What counts is a new creation.' There is more to salvation than only forgiveness, only justification. There is also sanctification. This might be where the modern apostasy comes in. It is the desire in many churches today to define exactly what that new creation will look like. Among the feminists, the new creation will look like feminism. Among the liberation theologians, the new creation will look like liberation activism. The New Right among us will slant sanctification toward a New Right activism. Apostasy might have to do with legalisms surrounding sanctification."

The specifically ecclesiological issue was again put forth—this time by Fr. Thomas Hopko of St. Vladimir's Orthodox Seminary. "The real issue is not sanctification, or the loss of authority, but the loss of the church as a communion in which in fact the new creation is an immediate experience to the believer by grace through faith, because there is real communion with God. The church, the city of God, should be experienced as a sacramental-mystical-communal institution that judges all ideologies and encourages engagement and insists on freedom not to identify with one or another. Therefore it produces the blood of the martyrs throughout history. Unfortunately, since the church has become invisible and individuals are justified by faith, the *polis* has become the church. The *polis* has become the only arena of Christian activity, because there is no church as church. Therefore, today getting the right politics is getting the right faith. In American Protestantism, ecclesiology becomes sociology and perhaps politics."

Berger complemented Hopko's emphasis on the church as church by directing attention to very practical, even pastoral, concerns. "Affirmation of the catholicity of the church translates itself empirically into a very simple question: Can I be in communion with those with whom I disagree politically? That question can be broken into two questions: Do I want to be in communion with those with whom I disagree politically? and Do they want me to be in communion with them? Generally I want to be in communion. But I do not want to be in communion with people who torture other people or who own slaves or who defend totalitarianism in absolute terms. Do I want to be in communion with people active in the South African disinvestment campaign? Of course. But do they want to be in communion with me? My limited Protestant experience has taught me that if I do not meet a checklist of about twelve political items, I am not in communion with them, as far as they are concerned. I am in fact excommunicated, and very often explicitly so. That is the root of the scandal. That is the theological-ecclesial issue which is the most serious of all."

Extending Berger's interest in the church's catholicity, Neuhaus wondered why some American bishops don't excommunicate members of their flock who dissent from their churches' current social-political positions. He picked on the United Methodists. "The United Methodist bishops issued a pastoral on war and peace in which they, in their own words, went farther than the Roman Catholic bishops. They were very forceful—so much so that they explicitly said that anyone who supports a policy of nuclear deterrence is an idolater and is worshiping a false god. That is very hard language. I have been in a number of sessions with some United Methodist bishops in which I've said that this is very strong language and asked if the bishops really mean it. If they do mean it, then, since 75 percent of the United Methodists in America voted for Ronald Reagan and, it may be assumed, probably support the general defense policies of his administration, why don't they excommunicate these people? Why don't the bishops have the nerve, the courage of their own position, to say that some of their flock are outside the church and worshiping a false god? Clearly, some kind of church discipline is in order. To which the United Methodists say, 'You're using a Lutheran or Roman Catholic understanding of the church. That is not what we mean by the church.' It is a very interesting statement."

Neuhaus pursued the matter of Protestant confusion on the meaning of the church, again picking on the United Methodists. "Wolfhart Pannenberg was in the United States visiting some time ago. He was spending a couple of days, for his sins, with a group of United Methodist clergy in California. Mainly he was listening to their conversation. Later he said about his days with the Methodists, 'This is very puzzling to me. They kept using the word *we*. They said, "*We* are wrong in doing that. *We* should do that. *We* have made a mistake here. *We* should repent of that." For two days—*we, we, we*. I sat there saying, Who is the *we*? Is it we Christians? Is it we Methodists? Is it we Americans? Who is the *we*? Then I discovered that the *we* was interchangeable. The *we* was all of the above.' That brings us back to the specifically American character of what may be an unconscious apostasy, deeply rooted in a typically American lack of any ecclesiology that could produce witnesses, never mind martyrs."

The Problem with the Seminaries

In a conference heavy with seminary professors, the subject of theological education today was bound to come up sooner or later. One of those professors, David Lotz, was the first to bring it up.

"Looking at theological education," said Lotz, "we are involved in education that has lost its coherence. The seminary catalog is a menu, a smorgasbord. There are no courses in my seminary, for example, called 'The Christian Gospel.' Instead you start out doing Bible and maybe the history of theology, but you do it sequentially, and you are immediately launched into very difficult problems of hermeneutics and of historical-critical studies. We don't talk about the gospel or the coherence of the theological enterprise. In my judgment the education is atomistic. We have lost the gospel in the theological enterprise. We have lost the church in church history. I am a church historian, but I don't talk about the church. I talk about the churches, which are approached in an institutional-phenomenological fashion. There are historical reasons for this. They are largely bound up in the modern mind and the historical-critical approach, which tell us that we cannot justify traditional theological language and appeals to the acts of God in history. That is left to theology. But the theologians don't talk about it either. There are serious problems in our theological training across the board."

Oden, who also teaches in a school of theology, then lamented that the atomization of theological education had allowed new orthodoxies to take root in the seminaries. Feminism, he said, is but one of the new orthodoxies. But the lamentations did not last long for Oden, for he envisioned the possibility of correction by the biblical tradition. "In Galatians," he began, "there is the phrase 'that which we have received.' It refers to the pre-Pauline apostolic tradition, what the community received from the outset of the postresurrection experience. In the modern seminary we have freedom to teach, but what we teach should not be contrary to 'that which we have received.' In other words, there is freedom of inquiry—but under those constraints. Classically, those constraints have been exercised through the episcopal teaching office and ordination and curricular decisions and faculty appointments in the seminaries.

"Also, there is tremendous wisdom in a neglected part of the New Testament—the pastoral epistles," Oden continued. "For a hundred years we have suffered under the notion that these later so-called catholicizing developments in the New Testament indicated a vast deterioration of the original vitality of Christianity. However, these epistles contain good theological intuition in trying to build a structure of surveillance, continuity, and maintenance for 'that which we have received.'"

As a sociologist, Berger was more interested in the description of than the prescription for the problem in the seminaries. He spoke out of experience: "At the Boston University School of Theology there is a New Class core curriculum. It may not be stated as such, but we know what it is, and it enters into every course. Those who push it have committee meetings, study sessions, and retreats to make sure it does enter into every course. That curriculum is liberationism in its various forms, especially a Sandinista-oriented leftism and a radical feminism. They have succeeded at Boston. And my impression is that it is not terribly different at other seminaries."

With that the conference was again reminded that the charge of apostasy of contemporary American churches had been placed squarely on the table. Not all agreed with the charge, but all respected it enough to wrestle with it. Now the conference prepared to dig through the historical record in search of possible sources of the alleged apostasy.

UNBELIEF IN AMERICA

James Turner's paper, which examines the historical roots of unbelief in America, was the second paper up for discussion. Turner, a Michigan historian, opened his segment of the conference with a plea for understanding. "We cannot regard the strategies which Protestant leaders in eighteenth- and nineteenth-century America adopted to secure belief as somehow contemptible. They were in a very awkward situation. In retrospect it is easy enough for us to point fingers and say they went wrong here or there. But they did not do such a bad job, given the circumstances under which they were working. They had somehow to bring religious beliefs that were couched philosophically in terms that were rapidly becoming antiquated into relationship with more modern currents of intellectual life. They had somehow to bring notions of the church's mission and role in the world, which had previously been geared to older forms of social structure, into some relationship with newer social structures that were emerging. Doing that is terribly complex. By and large, the strategies they adopted look pretty good in the context of the time they were working in."

To this, Richard Neuhaus responded with tongue in cheek: "Well, the cat is out of the bag. We can all see what Jim Turner is up to. He's trying to suck us into taking a charitable view of things. That is a very, very troubling direction." Loud laughter ensued.

Undaunted, Turner extended his plea for understanding and for the recognition of complexity: "If you read histories written around 1700 and then you read histories written around 1850, you will find that usually they are about political events. But they are remarkably different stories. Those written around 1700 emphasize in their explanation of political events very personal sorts of motivations—for example, greed, ambition, and so on. Their story of political development is the story of individuals in conflict with each other while seeking to realize their aims by various and nefarious means. Historical understanding is filled with conspiracies, because that is the kind of category that makes sense. If you read histories written around 1850, you walk into a different world. Their explanatory categories tend to be social rather than individual. Economic forces begin to play a major role. Even the more personalistic sorts of motives tend to be embodied not in the ambitions of individuals but in the collective thinking of groups. There is, in short, a shift in causation from the individual and personal to the social.

"We owe that in part to people like Marx. We owe it much more, I think, to the Scottish Enlightenment. But once the social becomes an explanatory category in history, it spills over into other areas of explanation, including theology. A Social Gospeler like Walter Rauschenbusch needs to be understood both in the context of a professionalizing society in which class structure is shifting and in the terms of the social form of explanation. The relationship of religious belief to social structure becomes far more complex."

Enough on understanding. Now Turner tackled one of the Social Gospelers' problems. "The Social Gospelers, who are liberal theologians in the late nineteenth century, gave their allegiance in terms of political method to social science. It is that batch of people that is most liable to secularization. Also, they tend to follow the leftward drift of the academy in the twentieth century and the leftward drift of the social sciences in particular. But many of those people are also drifting out of Christianity, or out of a vital relationship to Christianity."

Finally, Turner wanted to know why. Why has Protestantism proved to be so liable to the corrosions—the temptations of unbelief, the leftism, and so on—that historical analysis suggests? He ventured that "the answer has to do with the specific nature of specific religious traditions—what is there in the tradition that pulls people together? In Roman Catholicism there is the church, as institution, as authority, and in its sacramental role. In Judaism there is a much longer shared history and an ethnic component that hold people to some kind of Jewish identity even when the pattern of their beliefs would suggest that there is no theological cohesion. I suspect the role of the church is critical to Orthodoxy." Precisely the role of the church as church, Turner implied, is largely absent throughout much of the history of American Protestantism.

Now it was Neuhaus's turn to plead for a little understanding—for the Social Gospelers: "Those who are often dismissed, especially the Social Gospelers, as being simply cultural accommodationists really did have a belief system about God's providential purpose in history and the role of this culture, this democratic experiment, in the unfolding of that purpose." Then he looked at the present scene. "Today there is a remarkable shift. For today the religious right seriously, in a theological way, tries to argue for the proposition of a Christian America in some sense or another and for the reconstituting of society on the basis of Bible, law, and so on. Why has that kind of belief about discerning providential purpose in this historical moment gravitated from left to right over the last hundred years?

"One might say that the unhappy results of the church running the risk of engaging culture are nothing new," Neuhaus continued. "One might say, 'What's so new or alarming about the present state of the church? Hasn't it always been this way, not only in American Christianity but also in two millennia of Christianity, with these kinds of ambiguities and compromises and sellouts of the gospel?' There is something attractive about that argument, about looking at the church in terms of centuries and not being panicked by the immediacy of our problems. But there is also something very deceptive about it, because it can easily suck us into a kind of complacency."

Finally, Neuhaus subtly sided with the party of alarm and against the party of complacency. "What if one said that this has always been the case in the church and that these engagements have always led to these risks and that these risks have frequently led to the problems about which we are concerned? Is that so alarming? It is if in the periods where these particular failures are rampant in terms of the selling-out of the gospel we really believe that people are being denied the joy of salvation and perhaps salvation itself."

Historical theologian David Lotz once again raised the issue of why American Protestantism took at least one wrong turn. "It seems that American Protestantism, according to Professor Turner, is always taking its cues from elsewhere and largely from outside the theological context. It is taking its cues from modernity, from the scientific revolution, and so on. What is left out there is the whole impress of modern theology from Schleiermacher onward, which understood Christianity as the letting loose in the world of a divine principle. The argument was that the Logos assumed not a specific man but human nature generically understood. This means, in principle, that human nature has been divinized, and it is now the task of the church to realize that which has already taken place in principle in the God-man himself. This is Schleiermacher. But also, this is Horace Bushnell."

Turner was unconvinced. "You have to remember how few Americans read German prior to the middle of the nineteenth century. Horace Bushnell becomes the first considerable American theologian to show the power of German historicism. But when does Bushnell start to publish significant works? It is almost 1850. So we are talking about German historicism coming into play in

American theology in a significant way only after mid-century, by which time this structure that I've been describing is already in place."

Thomas Hopko joined Lotz in claiming to see something more in the religious history of America than Turner was seeing. "Perhaps something else is going on in the nineteenth century—not just a divinization of modern science and social reform. It is amazing that every religious group that came to America in the nineteenth century had the same rhetoric, claiming something about America allegedly on the basis of its pure understanding of theology. They say, 'Finally in America we have a place that our theology can be lived out.' So what happens is that the idea develops that America is somehow called, it somehow has a destiny, it somehow is special in God's plan." According to Hopko, the Deists did this. The Puritans did this. And most other religious groups did this.

Turner agreed with Hopko's comment and then recast it in the terms of denominationalism. "What people often forget is that the United States invented denominationalism. It was in the United States that the churches were first disestablished to a significant extent. That created a series of problems for the churches, particularly for New England Congregationalism and Presbyterianism and others that had strong traditions of being state churches and of having the accompanying influence. The response of the churches was to try to fill that void—and this is exemplified by Lyman Beecher and other revivalist social reformers—by attaching the church to the nation, as a voluntary organization. The mission of the church then comes to be the transformation of the nation by Christianizing the nation—not only redeeming the nation for Christ but reestablishing the centrality of the church. Disestablishment is crucial in this American sense of a special social mission."

The Church and Modernity

Given the strong nineteenth-century attractions of social science, social activism, German theologies, and manifest destinies, how was the American church to chart its course in American society? Furthermore, how should it chart that course today?

The first task of the church, said Ernest Fortin, is defensive in nature. "If you accept the scientific premise, it is difficult to defend the things that Christianity traditionally stands for—virtue, dedication to others, family values, education, and so on. In modernity you are talking about a universe in which there simply isn't any room for these things. You can talk about them and long for them, but how can you make them stick? They are not plausible. The modern world is the sort of world that doesn't accommodate any purpose."

Sometimes—in fact far too often—the Christian defense has become a Christian defensiveness, Steinfels noted: "Christians have always had a tendency to take refuge in the gospel and refuse to see the world around them."

Peter Berger shot back, "Possibly, but I don't think that that is our problem today."

"But it was a real problem in the Catholic Church until about twenty years ago," Steinfels insisted. "The Catholic Church is now struggling with the very issue that Protestantism has struggled with for some time."

This brought Berger to clarify his position: "Let me stipulate that there are historical situations and individuals in any historical moment associated with the great temptation to turn away from the world into some sort of pietistic contemplation, taking leave from the public challenges of the day. I would argue that that is not our major problem today in American Christianity."

In his paper and earlier in the discussion, Turner had postulated that one of the tasks of the church is very clear: it must either attempt something like apologetics and engage modernity or else face irrelevance in the modern world. In other words, said Turner, "Christianity has to come to intellectual terms with modernity. If the church does not do that, its faith ends up in somebody's cultural attic. The problem in the history of justifications of Christian truthclaims is not the attempt to find intellectual defenses for Christianity; the problem is the loss of balance in doing so. The problem is not that Christians were responding to modernity; the problem is that they surrendered to modernity."

Hopko added that "throughout church history it has never been a question of the gospel's engagement with the prevailing definitions of reality. The real issue is who is doing it right and who isn't, who is faithful and who isn't. Already in the New Testament canon the claim is made that Matthew, Mark, Luke, John, Paul, and so on were all doing it right, and a lot of literary people were not. But it is not simply a case of doing it or not doing it."

Hopko went on to question the cool, calm, and calculated model of Christian engagement. "It is not historically justifiable to claim, as is popularly done, that since Gregory of Nyssa lived in the fourth century, he had to communicate with the Hellenistic world, and therefore he chose certain categories. I think that is total nonsense! Gregory was simply alive at that time, and his language and his culture were Hellenistic, so in Hellenistic terms he was trying to say what he believed to be true. The subsequent church tradition said that on these issues he was right and on these he was wrong."

Hopko concluded by discussing what successful engagement is all about. "In the Orthodox tradition there are those who are successful in the sense that they are not apostate—the Church Fathers, the saints. But humanly speaking, these have never been successful in the public sphere. They are minorities, often persecuted minorities. To say that there was ever a 'success' of Orthodox Christianity in history is not correct. Gregory of Nyssa gave his five theological orations on the Trinity, which now we praise and teach, in a room smaller than this one, and to fewer people." Success based on faithfulness, according to Hopko, runs counter to the compulsions of modern Western Christianity, which appears to lust after acceptance from the cultured elite who despise it and which seems to depend on an array of secular justifications.

While recognizing the necessity of the church's apologetic task, Avery Dulles indicated that "apologists through history have tended to fail. This is their professional weakness, because they do not offer the needed correctives. They fall into the categories they are using and give their audience too much of what it expects, without the surprising good news. Perhaps this is the failure of liberation theologians—they are falling into the categories of Marxist social analysis without correcting them sufficiently."

Looking for a vigorous swim against the stream, Ken Myers questioned even the necessity of Christian apologetics. "In Paul's second letter to Timothy, he states that there will come a time when apostasy will be in vogue, when people will not hear the truth and will listen to myths instead. In such a time the attempt to establish a new synthesis between faith and culture is a very dangerous one, and therefore Paul does not enjoin Timothy to try to establish a new synthesis. Instead, he tells Timothy and the others to be sober and faithful to what they were taught." Perhaps, Myers was suggesting, this is such a time for the church in America. Perhaps the church should not be scrambling to assemble yet another synthesis. Perhaps the church should be content with being faithful to "that which we have received." Perhaps.

It was then that Carl Braaten described the present breakdown in American Christianity. "American Christianity's synthesis is now coming apart. We are moving into a new time. Some call it the post-Christian or postmodern age. I'm not sure about the nature of our time, but we are in serious doubt about the modern synthesis of

Christianity and scientific epistemology. There is a restlessness, and I certainly participate in it. Many are calling for a new paradigm for theology today."

Then Braaten issued a challenge to the church to charge into the future: "How will we be able to reestablish Christian identity in the emerging new situation without referring to the third, fourth, or fifth centuries? Because those were particular Christian-cultural amalgamations for their times. I hope that we have an alternative other than trying to restore or repristinate the Christian syntheses of the ancient world. We cannot hanker to go back. We must go forward. We must find how to 'read the signs of the times.' It is useful to sit in judgment of the past, but now we are in charge. We are responsible, as Christians today, for relating the gospel to our time. We cannot retreat to eternity or to another world. I believe the gospel is incarnate in this world in Jesus and in the apostolic words and in the actions that emanated from their belief. We have always had the gospel intersecting in a kind of asymmetrical way with any particular age. This is what we are looking for now."

Not surprisingly, historian Turner upheld tradition, all of Christian tradition, as a key to the American church's future. "We cannot believe that we will find Christian identity in the fourth or fifth century. We have to look at the whole sweep of tradition in trying to find a Christian identity from which American Christianity can come to terms with our own cultural situation. I would only hope that we don't forget that the seventeenth, eighteenth, nineteenth, and indeed the first part of the twentieth century are also part of the church's tradition, though because we are so much closer to them in time they appear much more fragmented, much more confusing than earlier centuries."

Referring to a book edited by Thomas Hopko on the ordination of women, Neuhaus said, "It often has happened in Christian history that great issues that had not been presented to the church in a specific form take the church by surprise. The church does not know how to respond. But intuitively, the church answers, 'This is wrong. We do not presently know how to articulate why it is wrong.'" However, in time, Neuhaus added, the church gets its act together. It gets over the initial surprise and then formulates a usually convincing and rational response to the new issue.

Modernity, in a way, took Christianity by surprise. Over the last two or three centuries, the church has had premodern phases, in which ecclesiastical authoritarianism prevailed. And the church has had modern phases, in which modernity's ideal of human autonomy won the day. Now the church is finally feeling its way, as if in the dark, toward a postmodernity. Postmodernity, urged Neuhaus, recognizes the "utter impossibility of living autonomously and of trying to find universalistic answers or criteria of judgment which are unconditioned by history, value-neutral, value-free, and rationally justifiable to all. The church is trying to determine what is authoritative for establishing the criteria of judgment." This conference, all of those around the table surely hoped, was an attempt to participate in the church's present struggle to formulate criteria of judgment that will seriously engage, while not capitulating to, the modern world.

Not Sensing Sin?

The church's encounter with modern America is certain to involve the category—and, needless to say, the reality—of sin. Glenn Tinder of the University of Massachusetts ably expressed this and more: "There is an American lack of a sense of sin. This may go along with a sense of guilt. This is a theme that Reinhold Niebuhr of course stated very strongly—that America lacks a sense that there is a fundamental derangement in human nature. This lack of a sense of sin may be particularly strong, for some reason, in the New Class. The political attitudes of the New Class might be caused or conditioned by its lack of a sense of sin, of a sense of the limitations on the possibilities of human action, and of a sense of the ambiguity of all political programs."

Then Tinder held forth on the sin of those who ignore sin. "The connection between faith and good works is strong, and we should not weaken it. It is Pauline, Lutheran, and so on—there are all kinds of authority for maintaining the closest possible connection between faith and works. Faith requires works, and it requires political works. And it seems to me that the political works toward which Christianity leans tend to the left, because of Christianity's inherent egalitarianism. However, social idolatry comes in when there is no sense that political works are done by sinful people in a sinful world. Sin means that every political program will fail, more or less."

Peter Berger was thoroughly unconvinced, and he said so. "If there is a lack of a sense of sin in American culture, why is there all of this guilt around? This is a tremendously guilt-prone culture. For example, on the current Iran-contra thing, some demand that Reagan should confess and apologize, and then presumably we would collectively give him absolution. This doesn't suggest a lack of a sense of sin. Could it be that we have a Pelagian sense of sin, rather than an Augustianian sense? Or could it be that we have a nontragic sense of the evils of this world?"

This sent Tinder back briefly to the drawing board. While there he came up with a statement on guilt: "Could we say that there is a great sense of guilt but not a conscious sense of self-guilt? In other words, people feel guilty, but they emphatically deny that they are guilty."

Speaking as a sociologist of guilt, Berger replied, "We are surrounded by people who are constantly willing to shoulder guilt, especially if we talk about the New Class. Its members are willing to accept guilt about anything. Some seem to imply, 'Pardon me for living. I am a white male fascist. Forgive me.' Where is this reluctance to shoulder guilt? I see an overwhelming readiness to accept guilt for things that a reasonable person would say I couldn't possibly be guilty of."

Then someone blurted out, "Guilt is supposed to make you feel bad. It makes these people feel good."

Neuhaus observed that "you don't feel good unless you feel bad."

A serious comment—and one that seems somewhat surprising when its Lutheran source is considered—interrupted the laughter. Said Berger, "The simplistic drama of guilt, repentance, and absolution is operating here."

Professor Jenson was now ready to speak about sin. "Protestants today are predominantly antinominian. That is to say, we are so tragic about sin that we cannot repent of anything in particular, nor can we stop doing it. That is what is peculiarly American about the sense of sin—not that it is so superficial, but that it is so deep. So we repent of the whole universe. That opens our moral judgments to being made according to whatever agenda we are fixed on. I don't have to consult the Ten Commandments to find out what to think about something, because I think I am already much deeper than that. I can plumb the depths—where it turns out that overthrowing the Sandinistas or supporting the Sandinistas is what really emerges. There is a peculiar connection between antinomianism and the freedom to proclaim agendas as the law of God."

"In terms of the nineteenth century, this sounds implausible," said the unconvinced Richard Neuhaus. "I don't think that in the nineteenth century the Methodists would have talked about being guilty of the universe."

Jenson defended his case by noting that "pietism has always done that sort of thing, and American Christianity has always been pietistic."

Persistent in getting back to the issue of America, Thomas Hopko brought it into the discussion of sin. "If it is in the American bloodstream, in our guts, that there is something special about America, that there is some kind of calling, some kind of manifest destiny, and that it is connected with things like egalitarianism, freedom, democracy, and so on—that is a pretty heavy burden to carry. It makes the gospel look like nothing. If that is the American role in the world—always to be right, always to be leading, always to be supporting the right side, and always being called to that— that can go a long way in explaining the guilt we are talking about. That is as much at the root of the guilt-ridden American as anything coming from the church or the synagogue. It is coming from the public school systems. They teach how everybody is equal, everybody is special, everybody is good. That has to be remembered. Also, the churches and synagogues have become lifestyle enclaves where people learn how to cope and feel right—to *feel* right about oneself and oneself in the world—rather than to *be* right. It's a global village now, so you've also got to feel right about Nicaragua, South Africa, and everywhere else."

Hopko's comment triggered a comment from Neuhaus. Throughout American history, he began, "There is a continuing sense of American singularity, exceptionalism, mission, providential purpose. But in the nineteenth century there was manifest destiny, the desire to be the city on the hill and the new order for the ages. From there you go, with an equal sense of responsibility or burden of being at the center of the cosmic unfolding of purposes, to America being the cancer of the world in the twentieth century. The enormous responsibility and burden of being American moves from a sense of high promise and participation in providential purpose to a sense of being the children of darkness. It moves from being the children of light to being the children of darkness. It moves from special privilege to a very special guilt."

Uses of the Truth

It was time for moderator Neuhaus to try to tie together the Berger and Turner papers. He suggested that the papers connected on the relationship between utility and truth. "Berger complains that the utility of religion, especially defined in social-political-cultural terms, ends up inevitably and inescapably an abuse of religion and indeed an eclipse of the authentic gospel. So, an important question arises: What is Christianity for? Is there some sense in which we legitimately and necessarily can talk out of the core sources of authentic gospel Christianity about what it is for, about what it is supposed to do, about what it is useful for? What are the contributions of Christianity with respect to the world, culture, society? What is it for?" Then Neuhaus confessed his own bias in the matter: "There are, I believe, legitimate ways in which you can talk about the justification of religious truth-claims. There is a legitimate relationship between utility and truth, but they must never be equated." Now it was up to the others to agree or disagree.

Not one to let others represent his position, Berger had this to say: "Instead of truth, I suggest that we discuss reality. This is why. Reality asserts itself by resisting us. It is there. It imposes itself as reality. It is inappropriate to ask how reality can be useful. Of course our utilitarian projects must reckon with reality, but that is quite different. Indeed, as soon as one asks how something can be used, one is already denying that this something is real, and one is justifying one's belief in this something. One doesn't have to justify belief in anything that is clearly real. These considerations refer to ordinary, mundane realities. It seems to me that they also refer to religious definitions of reality and truth-claims.

"Gregory of Nyssa, Thomas Aquinas, Hegel—none of them reinterpreted Christianity in terms of a pragmatic agenda," Berger went on. "All of them were concerned with reinterpreting the truth of Christianity—not its utility—in the categories of their own times. The problem we face today is very different from earlier intellectual syntheses."

Oden tried his hand at joining the Berger and Turner papers: "Ironically, both of these papers are concerned with justification. Professor Berger's paper centers on man's being made righteous before and by God—that is, it centers on man's justification before and by God. Professor Turner's paper focuses on reasons for validating or justifying the Christian faith in the modern world. Obviously, the two presumed contexts or audiences differ. Berger's paper discusses justification before God; Turner's explores a justification before the public, before society."

Methodism, said Oden, addressing public justification, has for generations employed a "quadrilateral" method for evaluating truth-claims: "Scripture, church tradition, religious experience, and reason make up the sides of this methodological quadrilateral. In the modern period, unfortunately, experience and reason have been retained while Scripture and tradition have been dropped. At the same time—and this is surely related to the retention of only experience and reason—there has been an unrelenting polemic carried out against the Bible and tradition in which it has been claimed that they do not have much to say in public." It might be noted that utility figures into the quadrilateral only insofar as it is considered a part of the side of reason. Oden seemed to be teaming up with Berger and challenging the wisdom of the Neuhaus question relating utility and truth.

Fortin was the third conferee to take a crack at the Neuhaus query: "The issue is not so much the utility of Christianity. You have to ask, in a prior way, why anybody would accept Christianity in the first place. Well of course if you are born in a Christian world and you received a Christian education, that would not be a pressing question. But what caused the Roman world to embrace this new and fantastic religion? There had to be something attractive in it. What did people see in it that they did not find elsewhere? Why did it conquer the world within a space of less than three centuries? How do you account for that? Of course there is divine providence and protection. Maybe that is the truth of it."

According to Werner Dannhauser, "the justification of Christianity by utility has really very little to do with Christianity. It can be and has been praised by political philosophers. They say that Christianity is false but very useful to have around."

"The noble lie," said Neuhaus.

Dannhauser then asserted that "among all the justifications of Christianity there is what has been called the brute fact of revelation. Was the tomb empty? The point is, Was Christ raised from the dead? The question of truth is preeminent in Christianity, even over the issue of utility. However, the notion of truth that is claimed for Christianity has shrunk tremendously in the last three centuries. So there is something wrong with Christian apologetics. It has been yielding a tremendous area to modern science. One of the reasons that Christianity became so moralistic is that it ceased to be cosmological. It yielded cosmology, and all of us are living with the consequences of that. We have a tacit or overt acceptance of the fact-value distinction, which has crept into all of our speech. It assumes there are two realms—fact and value—and that religion has very little to say about the realm of facts. And it assumes that social science is quasiautonomous and that there is a neutral world out there. This has worked to the great detriment of religion in general. Also it has led to something that is new in modernity—the claim for the moral grandeur of atheism, that atheism has a kind of integrity, a kind of facing things down to the last consequence that is not possible for believers."

Turner, a historian of atheism in America, objected: "In retrospect it is not entirely clear that that is true."

Wasting no time, Dannhauser let another opinion fly in Turner's direction: "That is part of a modern problem regarding history. Moderns are implicitly driven to claim to understand the seventeenth century better than the seventeenth century understood itself. I do not think that is a Christian view. It is a very problematic view."

Yes, said Turner, but "it is a view that makes historical writing possible. Historians have always held that view." Nonhistorians might call it the historian's occupational hazard.

Robert Jenson then proceeded to play his Barthian card: "The neo-orthodox scheme distinguished the Christian gospel from the Christian religion. On the Christian gospel I want to say everything that Peter Berger has said. Indeed, according to the Reformation, the gospel is that creative Word of God by which he creates the world in the first place and continues to create us as we hear it. So, the question of its utility is indeed absurd. On the other hand, the Christian religion is the collection of practices, affiliations, social groupings, and ideologies that comes into being as people hear the gospel in particular contexts. Here the question of utility can very well and legitimately be posed. There are many necessary interests which will be better served if the Christian religion flourishes than if it does not. And one of them is surely the one that appears in the title of this conference—namely, the ordering of our lives, temporal and eternal. The Christian religion is surely our attempt to respond to the revelation of the eternal and to order our lives to it. The phenomenon which occasions this conference is the attempt of Christian religionists—forget about the gospel now—to order life in this world without direct reference to that gospel."

Reinforcing Jenson's distinction between the Christian gospel and the Christian religion, Carl Braaten remarked, "Kierkegaard claimed that while Luther had ninety-five theses, he had only one, which was that New Testament Christianity does not exist in this world. He said you cannot have Christianity established as something official, with the pastors and leaders earning their living by it, because they are then relying on the world to provide them with props and supports. That was a very serious indictment against the Christianity of his time. The leaders of the church then were doing their jobs, preaching the Word of God, administering the sacraments, and so on, but it was Kierkegaard's perception that something had come apart." Whatever else had come apart, Kierkegaard wanted to sunder Christian truth from perceptions of how it might be immediately useful, and to this day he stands in solemn judgment against casual concoctions of usefulness and Christian truth.

The Unity and the Disunity of the Gospel

Beginning a comment that would redirect the conference conversation, David Lotz said, "What continues to bother me is on what grounds we determine what is apostasy. With reference to what? The assumption is that the gospel is something we can identify and that it is homogeneous."

Lotz went on to explain: "A canon must exclude, divide, discriminate. In the canons to which we appeal in the Christian community and in the academic community—the sciences, humanities, and so on—there is increasingly a lack of the necessary agreement and uniformity and homogeneity that constitute canons. Theologians—biblical, exegetical, systematic, and practical—are using the Christian message or gospel as the proverbial wax, which they mold as they will."

Neuhaus summarized the concerns of fellow Lutheran Lotz: "There is today no agreement on the gospel canon."

Lotz could not have agreed more. "Well, all right. The words *Scripture* and *history* presuppose homogeneity. The difficulty today is that Scripture cannot function any longer as a canon, in the traditional sense, apparently because one can find in the Scriptures justifications for positions that traditionally were thought to be excluded. So we end up with the canon in the canon, or canons within the canon. The same thing might be extended to the other disciplines, the so-called secular disciplines—within history, for example. Today in the reviews in the journals we've got the social historians taking it out on the theological historians. We've got the econometric historians. We've got the psychohistorians. The trouble is that because of this disunity regarding the scriptural canon, the Scriptures can no longer witness in truth and in power. And because the Scriptures can no longer witness," Lotz concluded, "other canons and other gospels rush in to fill the void."

Berger wanted to make something perfectly clear to the conferees: "I was not assuming homogeneity. I was assuming there is something real, transcendentally real, to which these different attempts at establishing a canon refer. As far as I have stuck my nose into New Testament scholarship, which is not terribly deep, that difficulty extends right into the New Testament itself. But that does not change the fact that all of these attempts were attempts to come to grips with something that was perceived as real, which is the event surrounding the phenomenon of Jesus Christ." Berger, then, located unity in the transcendent, in Christ, and not in the witnesses to or the canons regarding the transcendent.

Interested in a scriptural unity of the gospel, Benestad spoke out of the Roman Catholic tradition: "Thomas More argued that you can't know what Scripture is apart from the church. Also, Augustine argued that if you find anything in Scripture which contradicts charity, it's wrong. How could he say that? Because somehow the tradition of the church helps us to interpret that book. In other words, that book is interpreted very differently from any ordinary book. I don't think we would say that about reading Plato or Shakespeare—that we have to read it in the light of some tradition. But that has been a historic claim of the church—to read the Bible in the tradition."

While the conference was on the issue of the canon, Fortin admitted that he did not know exactly who put the New Testament books together but that whoever it was must have been fairly intelligent, because "he chose the books that I would have chosen." Laughter, led by the self-effacing Fortin, ensued.

After the chuckles died down, Peter Berger took one more cut at the unity question: "Unity becomes visible when one has a certain distance from what is being observed. I realize what it is to be an American when I go abroad, for example. In an interesting way, I think that in this part of the twentieth century it is easier for us to see the unity in different Christian approaches because we now have a much smaller world, with much more intercultural communication. It is possible for us to look at ourselves through non-Western cultures and non-Western religions. That has been my major experience over the last twenty years because my work has been in the Third World.

"I heard a lecture recently by an historian of Central Asia on the incredible syncretistic phenomenona that took place in that region in the first centuries of the Christian era. It involved Christianity, Manichaeanism, Buddhism, Zoroastrianism—an unbelievable mixture. For example, he showed a beautiful picture of Jesus that came from what is now Soviet Central Asia. It showed an old Chinese gentleman with a beard, a Confucian scholar's robe; in his left hand he held a Manichaean cross and his right hand was lifted in a benediction gesture of the Buddha. He said often when you start reading texts from that period, you don't know if it is a Buddhist or a Christian text, because they are all mixed up. However, there is one thing, and when you find it, you always know that it is Christian. That is the physical resurrection of the dead.

"If there is a core, if there is a unity, if there is a historical and original confession of faith, it is that Jesus Christ is risen from the dead. This living core of what the gospel is can become visible to us today in a very refreshing way because we have the rich possibility today of encountering non-Christian interpretations of reality."

It was fitting, a little surprising, and perhaps providential for a discussion of unbelief, apologetics, sin, utility and truth, and gospel canon to end with a somewhat strong reference to the resurrection of Jesus. That reality always creates hope. And given the realities in the churches and the world today, hope unfortunately is often in very short supply.

THE CATHOLIC CASE

During the first day of conversation, the conference had not unanimously agreed on a definition of apostasy. Nor had the conferees uniformly affirmed the proposition that many churches in America have lapsed into apostasy, whatever its definition. But one thing was clear. All of those present were firmly convinced that many churches and denominations in America have a problem, a serious problem, a theological problem, which in its most extreme manifestations might be called apostasy.

It is, of course, not enough simply to describe and lament such a sad state of ecclesial affairs. Construction—or reconstruction—is necessary. In his paper and in his conversation, Fr. Avery Dulles, in the view of many Americans Catholicism's preeminent theologian, nudged the conference to look beyond a worrisome status quo toward the challenge of the church's constructive role in the ordering of life, temporal and eternal.

"The focus of my paper is on the official stance of the Roman Catholic Church, especially in the contemporary United States, and especially as expressed in statements of the National Conference of Catholic Bishops," Fr. Dulles began. "If one is looking for heresy or apostasy, these official statements, in my opinion, do not provide an example. They do not propose another way of salvation in addition to the faith once for all delivered to the saints. That is not to say there is not apostasy in other places.

"The gospel can never be reduced to politics. Life cannot be totally politicized. Against a politicized Christianity, I hold that all human beings, regardless of their social-political situation, are called to an immediate personal relationship with God and that their response to that call is decisive for eternal salvation. Today, even the church is in danger of forgetting or muffling the urgency of this call to eternal life. That puts the church dangerously close to irrelevancy and incredibility.

"On one level, Jesus showed a sublime unconcern for political relationships. I hold that the primary responsibility of the church is to announce the gospel of the kingdom by proclamation through word and symbolic action. The church's greatest contribution to the

political order may be the conviction it imparts that politics is not ul-
timately decisive because the gospel is. Only if politics is radically
relativized can certain political problems be handled.

"On a second level, the church must not only announce the
gospel but also respond to it corporately and individually. This is
where I see the distinction between gospel and law. The law can be
understood in terms of what the gospel requires us to do. This may
coincide with the work of sanctification. Whatever we hold about
the gospel and law, Christians are required to obey the Commandments and sincerely repent for their failures to live up to the Commandments. The church must accept the responsibility of helping its
members to live up to the demands placed on them, both personally and as members of society."

Dulles concluded his introduction on a biblical note. "If the
church gets too much into the area of trying to settle controversies
between opposed groups in the political arena, it can easily distract
us from the message of Jesus. Last night I was looking at the Gospel
of Luke, and I fell upon chapter 12. There someone in the crowd says
to Jesus, 'Teacher, tell my brother to give me the share of our in-
heritance.' This is a very reasonable request. Jesus replied, 'Friend,
who has set me up as your judge or arbiter?' Then he said to the
crowd, 'Avoid greed in all its forms; a man may be wealthy, but his
possessions do not guarantee him life.' I would like to hear a little
more of this when the bishops are speaking of the economic and social order. That is not to say that the church should not have social
teaching but rather that such teaching should not be its primary
message."

Unable to resist the temptation to comment on a strange turn in
conference logistics, Richard Neuhaus offered this commentary: "It
is piquant, to use one of John Courtney Murray's favorite words,
that we are now meeting at the Princeton Club with the A.C.L.U.
having its meeting next door. In some ways this juxtaposition is a
Christ-against-culture illustration, at least in terms of the presuppositions that are active there. And yet it is not unambiguously so,
because there are many things that have to do with human rights,
the dignity of the person, the democratic process, and so on, in
which we would see convergences between the directions they are
headed and the directions we would favor."

Law-Gospel Tensions

It took very little time for Protestant-Catholic tensions to surface.
Often these tensions were expressed in terms of law and gospel. For

example, Neuhaus noted that "Dulles uses law and gospel in a way that is troubling to many of us Lutherans, but not only Lutherans. Roman Catholics often talk about law as gospel and about laypeople needing guidance to act in accord with gospel teaching. To us and to others that is jarring."

But then, having not used up his weekly supply of charity, Neuhaus qualified his pointed point: "At least the first part of the Dulles paper makes clear that in the gospel, in the terms of the four Gospels, there is very little direct guidance with respect to behavior in the public arena. Or one might say that the guidance that is there is filled with contradictions, shocks, and inner tensions."

Another convinced Lutheran, Carl Braaten, noticed the same problem. "We have in Father Dulles's paper," he said, "a law-gospel problem. Maybe there is not such a great consensus between Lutherans and Catholics on justification. Maybe the official consensus is a contrived consensus, the appearance of consensus."

To this rather startling suggestion Dulles responded by recounting his experience in the Lutheran–Roman Catholic ecumenical dialogue. There, he recalled, law and gospel and faith and works had been discussed in depth. "We believed the theological disagreements in the dialogue to be serious," said Dulles, "but we were not sure that they were, of themselves, sufficiently grave to warrant a separation or mutual excommunication of the communities, because we could say a number of things in common and together about the gospel." The dialogue had ended up with a statement of convergence, not consensus.

At this point Tom Oden worried aloud about the contemporary similarities of—not tensions between—Catholicism and Protestantism that he perceived. "I want to state a sense of loss and pathos that I feel as a Protestant in relation to post–Vatican II developments. Others also, I am sure, feel this way. I happened to be in St. Peter's Basilica as a visitor at the time the Council was debating *Gaudium et spes*. I was one of the most enthusiastic about the series of events. But before Vatican II, Protestants, even though we existed in a relation of greater tension with Roman Catholics, had something against which to contend. It was solid. It was always there. Our very identity as Protestants was defined by the fact that we had something to protest against. Now, with all of the ambiguous achievements of Vatican II, which I think is a kind of protestantization (and I know that is unhappy language for many Roman Catholics), one feels that the mistakes that Protestants have spent four hundred years making are beginning to be made in a couple of decades by Roman Catholics. There is a kind of post–Vatican II malaise among Protestants in which we now realize that we must take up a kind of responsibility that we no longer see present in the solidity we once knew was in the Roman Catholic tradition. I experience that as a tremendous challenge, but more as a loss, as if something has gone out of my life."

Neuhaus picked up on another point of Lutheran-Catholic tension, regarding vocation. "Peter Berger is saying to the Catholic bishops, 'What are you doing chopping in my woodpile—on economics, on global development?' All the while, he is writing books and spending his life worrying about economics and what is good for the poor. Avery Dulles is not. Father Dulles is talking and working as a theologian, and he disclaims any knowledge as to social applications." Yet Neuhaus inferred that the bishops, talking and working as the spiritual and moral leaders of the church, certainly lay out some social applications of their own.

The discussion had been heavy with Luther's doctrine of the two kingdoms, however interpreted. On this doctrine Lutherans and many other Protestants could be expected to offer varying degrees of assent and Catholics could be expected to offer varying degrees of dissent. But things did not come out quite so neatly.

Glenn Tinder said, "I have been surprised at how sharply some of us have been making the distinction between the two kingdoms." This was a nice way of suggesting that the Lutherans were being too Lutheran. He then told about a recent visit to the University of Chicago Divinity School. The paper he presented had to do with religion and politics, and it was attacked in various ways by its audience. When Tinder had mentioned to the assembly that a modified two-kingdoms doctrine had informed his paper, the audience responded with an Aha! as if it had obtained a plea of guilty from a criminal suspect. He reported that the experience had only served to reinforce his two-kingdom conviction.

However, Tinder admitted, "Now I am finding that my adherence to the two-kingdoms doctrine is quite qualified. I am coming out of this conference with a sense that the gospel is replaced not only when it is identified with a political program but also when it is severed absolutely from the political world. I am going out of this conference with a sense of the creative demands and power of the gospel, which extend even into the political world. I am left with the sense that there are many profound issues in which the gospel makes particular political demands. For example, on totalitarianism. Is it impossible or is it invalid for the church to say that a Christian cannot be a member of the Communist Party? Or in the 1930s would it have been wrong for the Christian churches to say that you cannot be a member of the Nazi Party? Granted, you cannot push such prescriptions drawn from the gospel into every issue."

Neuhaus responded: "We are much more confident about what the church can say No to. The Nazi ideology contains much about the nature of the person and community that contradicts the Christian understanding of reality. Therefore, the church can clearly say that that understanding of the person and community and reality is incompatible with the gospel. It would then be a pastoral judgment, relative to the community of character, as to whether the church would authoritatively say, 'You cannot be a member of the Party.'"

Another Lutheran, David Lotz, wondered why opposition to the Nazi Party would have to be derived from the gospel, strictly understood. Tinder answered that opposition to the Nazi Party might come from the Gospels, but also from natural law and the Ten Commandments.

Lotz then moved in the Catholic direction: "What I am trying to advocate is not a separation between two kingdoms but an attempt to hold them in their appropriate tension. I want not only to distinguish between them carefully but also to allow for more of the transformationist motif within the realm of the kingdom of this world. But what does the gospel do? The gospel is the power of God unto salvation. Therefore, it supplies motivation. It gives me a vision of my life and the way in which I should order my life within society."

Neuhaus complained that Lotz was defecting from the Lutheran side of the debate. Lotz reassured him that he was simply rejecting Berger's apparently absolutist separation of the two kingdoms.

Presbyterian Richard Lovelace cast his vote with Lotz. "In studying the history of renewal, I have found that it is not just the Calvinistic tradition that has been activist in the realm of social justice. You find it among Lutheran pietists as well. They seem to overwhelm the two-kingdom teaching. Whether they have reasons for it or not, the heart along with Scripture propels them into making certain stands that are political and economic in nature."

Catholic University's Carl Peter stepped back, looked at the big picture, and added some much-needed perspective to the conversation. "I think every Christian has to walk a tightrope, and probably our institutions do too. The tightrope is between two sins—and they are both apostasy. One is idolatry, the other is blasphemy. Idolatry confuses the realm of the divine with the realm of the creaturely. That is the Catholic temptation. Blasphemy separates the two, and says that what God has done in declaring and making one just and holy has in fact not happened. It is speaking with insolence and arrogance regarding the divine works and is demeaning them. That is the Lutheran temptation. Catholics are concerned about blasphemy and that it not be allowed to go unchallenged."

Since Berger's allegedly too-separationist understanding of the two-kingdom doctrine had taken quite a beating that morning, he was allotted a considerable amount of time for response. Speaking to the concerns of Tinder and others, he said, "Let me take the case of totalitarianism, and the communist case rather than the Nazi case, because we know the outcome of the Nazi case and we do not know the outcome of the communist case. I think it is perfectly correct for the church as church to condemn totalitarianism in all of its forms. People may have different theological rationales for this—law, gospel, kingdom of reason, kingdom of grace, the Ten Commandments, and so on. There is every good reason for saying that the church should say that this is a form of regime which is not acceptable and must be condemned.

"Fine. But what do I do if I am a Christian in a totalitarian situation? In terms of my own cultural background, I find it easiest to imagine myself a citizen of the German Democratic Republic, which is a totalitarian state. At the moment it is not a terribly bloodthirsty one, but still it is a totalitarian state. I have given some thought to this. After all, I come from central Europe, and that fate could easily have happened to me.

"Let me shock you by saying that I think—I am not sure about this, but I think—I might want to join the Communist Party or the Socialist Unity Party of East Germany. I would do that without assent to communist ideology. But prudentially, it seems to me that the most likely change is going to come from modifications within the communist elite. I don't want World War III to happen in order to liberate my country. I don't want to foster armed insurrection against Soviet power, because I suspect that this is a hopeless undertaking. If I want any change at all, I probably have to work in the existing power structure. Now, I am not saying this is what I would do. I am just hypothesizing that prudentially this might be a conclusion that I would arrive at. I have a hunch, however, that I would arrive at that conclusion if I lived in Leipzig.

"Well, what do I do? I join the Communist Party. In order to do so, I certainly involve myself in evil. In fact I involve myself in a totalitarian situation which my church has just condemned. I feel that this is my obligation as a Christian in that particular historical situation. Now, in order to join the Communist Party, I would certainly have to lie, specifically lie about my Christianity. I'd sneak off to church with a hat pulled over my head so that I would not be seen. In other words, I'd be involved in an extremely ambivalent and ambiguous enterprise as a Christian. My political vocation, let us hypothesize, would have taken me there.

"What then would the church do for me, assuming that on Sundays I sneak off to worship in a church where they don't know me. I think I know what the church would do for me. It would do two very important things for me. One, it would assure me of forgiveness. Despite all these pretty awful things I'm involved in—probably not murder, but pretty unsavory stuff—the church will assure me of God's grace. The other thing the church will do for me is remind me that beyond all of the madness and horror of history there is something else—the coming kingdom of the risen Christ, which is cosmological, nonhistorical, and transcends all of the crap I'm involved in as a political actor. The less political the church is, the more it can do these two things for me. The more metapolitical the church is, the more it can do these things for me.

"Thank God I do not live in East Germany. I live in a democracy where there are all kinds of possibilities that I would not have over there. I don't think the basic formula is different, however. It is different in degree, but it is not different in kind. Even if I live in a democracy, the less political the church is, the more it can do for me."

Social and Antisocial Teaching

To put it bluntly, Roman Catholics are into social teaching. The law-gospel distinction and the two-kingdoms doctrine do not keep Catholics away from their social teaching. It is understandable, then, that Avery Dulles, in written and spoken word, focused much attention on Catholicism's social instruction and on the church's insistence on obedience to biblical commandments.

All of this talk about the social teaching of the church made Peter Berger a little nervous. "On whether there should be a social teaching of the church, I frankly disagree with Father Dulles. There is no way of reaching agreement on this, because in the self-understanding of the Roman Catholic Church there must be such teaching. I do not believe in the magisterial function of the episcopate. Frankly, I am not interested in what Roman Catholic bishops have to say about social matters. I do not see that they have any particular competence on these matters. That might be a prior Protestant prejudice. What they have in fact said I find extremely unhelpful."

"But Peter," Neuhaus noted, "you are interested enough in it to write about it."

All right, conceded Berger, "*interest* is perhaps the wrong word.

One has to be interested in what an important segment of the religious leadership of the nation says. President Reagan may not have anything useful to say, but since he is president of the United States I have to listen to him when he speaks. Let me try it again: I do not believe that what Roman Catholic bishops have to say about social matters is helpful to me, or helpful to anyone who wishes to understand the world."

Then Berger asserted: "Looking at what the Roman Catholic bishops have said, I would not for a moment accuse them of apostasy. My quarrel with them is that they are promoting bad economics, bad politics, and bad sociology. Therefore my quarrel with them is moral rather than theological."

James Turner, concerned that the meat ax was being applied to the social teaching of the church, addressed Berger: "Peter, you have said that there are circumstances in which the churches ought to make authoritative statements. An example comes to mind—Germany in the 1930s. So, where does one draw the line? What do you mean when you say the church should not have a social teaching?"

"You are right," Berger replied. "The church should say that anti-Semitism is a sin against God and man. And the church should stand against racism. But this social teaching is very negative. It is a prophetic condemnation of evil in society. I have no problem with that. There is very strong biblical warrant for saying this is what the church ought to do."

Then, as requested, Berger drew the line. "I do not think it is the church's business to enter into specific political agendas—by saying that one should vote for this bill, or by supporting this movement. But also it is not the church's business to enter into societal design. I do not think the church has a blueprint in any shape or form about what a good society would look like. When the church has done that, the results have generally been very unhelpful."

At this point Richard Lovelace took sides: "From a Reformed theological background, I find myself agreeing more with Father Dulles's position. In the Calvinist tradition there is a very vigorous assertion of the need to apply consistently biblical principles to personal ethics and to the social order. If you believe that Jesus is the Messiah and that he has a ruling function, then certainly there is a driving motivation to seek to extend the rule of Christ within society—although one has to take a strong dose of Reinhold Niebuhr in looking at the past results of such attempts to influence society. But where would we be in this country without the political assault on slavery that came out of the Second Great Awakening? Evangelists like Charles Finney made that possible. To be sure, the results were ambiguous and problematic, and we are still dealing with them. We dealt with them in part with another great Christian leader, Martin Luther King, Jr., who attempted to deal with real political-social issues of our day on the basis of the gospel of forgiveness and also on the basis of some biblical motifs."

But Berger retaliated: "Yes, historically Calvinism helped to bring about an end to slavery, but it also helped to bring about some less desirable things, such as arrogant American imperialism which held that America has a mission to do all sorts of things in the world. This can be chalked up to misunderstood Calvinism. But things are always misunderstood."

Steinfels offered a new argument for the social teaching of the church. "For the church to have no social teaching whatsoever is, in effect, to have a social teaching. The effect is to bless the status quo in which the church finds itself. Sometimes that is all right, and sometimes it is not.

"There is a good example in New York City of the gospel and social teaching. It concerns the corporal works of mercy by a number of churches in the city that have shelters for the homeless. That is a very simple response to a need caused by the lack of low-cost housing in New York City and throughout the metropolitan area. Knowing some people who work in them, I also know that doing this Christian service has led them to certain kinds of political thinking about the problem. It is no great surprise, then, that when legislation appears before the city council to preserve single-room-occupancy housing you find the majority of the proponents of this to be church people. That seems to me to be a highly specific political judgment on the part of church people, including laity and clergy. They started out performing a simple service—providing shelter for the homeless—and it drew them on to certain kinds of political and social thinking that is based in the gospel, on to fairly specific lobbying for certain legislation. I am hard-pressed to see why they should not be carrying out this agenda, given the enormity of the problem."

Berger had a problem with Steinfels's first point about no social teaching in fact being a social teaching. "I am not sure that is quite correct," he said. "It is not correct in ordinary life. If I say nothing, that does not necessarily mean that I agree with you. Lots of times I say nothing when I violently disagree with what people are saying. Silence does not mean assent. The only thing it does mean is that the status quo is not so awful that I felt constrained to voice my disapproval. Several congregations of the Confessing Church did one very quiet but enormously powerful thing, at least to anyone accustomed to the liturgy which was practiced in those churches. They simply omitted the prayer for the authorities. That was all. This was an enormous protest in that context against the legitimacy of the Nazi state. That was a thunderous protest.

"The prophetic mission of the church," the BU sociologist formulated, "should be exercised (a) rarely, (b) negatively, and (c) not in terms of propagating projects, programs, and so on."

Turning to Steinfels's second concern, Berger said, "Here it is important to distinguish diaconate from politics. Opening church buildings to house people who have no roof over their heads is a direct exercise of Christian love. In my opinion, this has no political implications. If the church should engage in politics on this issue, it is entering a quagmire. That is precisely the kind of thing it should not do. I do not know much about housing policy, but I do know that rent control is a powerful factor in making housing scarce. Do you really want the churches in New York City to organize and push for the abolition of rent control? I don't.

"Consider deinstitutionalization. A large factor in the homeless problem in the United States today is people deinstitutionalized from mental hospitals. The movement to do that, especially in New York, was an extremely admirable, humanitarian movement. No question about that. It tried to get people out of those snake pits, like Willow Brook on Staten Island. Who could quarrel with that? But some of the results have been disastrous. That is exactly what happens if you take a particular political agenda and say this is the way to go, for then you are responsible for the disaster that happens. If you are politically active in the world, you cannot avoid that. That is the tragedy of politics. There is no way of avoiding disasters. You have to act, however, as wisely as you can. I do not see why bishops ard church organizations enter this realm of tragic uncertainty, take one of several courses of action, and say that this is how Christians ought to go. They have neither competence nor authority to do that."

Neuhaus asked if the church's works of mercy should be considered a permanent ministry or a temporary stopgap measure until a just society takes over the works.

Steinfels replied, "It doesn't take very much imagination or analysis for someone volunteering in a shelter to see that that is no way for people to live, even if you think the church should be permanently in the business of running shelters. People deserve better."

"Of course," said Berger, "if I am a Christian who is also a citizen of the United States, and I am concerned about the homeless, I will want to do something politically about the problem. There is not a shred of disagreement about this. As far as the church as a community of Christians is concerned, I think it is very important that people on the left who believe that the answer to this problem is more public housing and people on the right who believe it to be the abolition of rent control—both with equal compassion for the homeless—should be able to worship together and not find that the church is aligned against them when they go there on Sunday morning. That is the issue, not that we have a political obligation. I take that for granted."

Catholic social teaching does have its advantages, contended Robert Jenson. After all, he urged, compare Catholicism and Protestantism today. "The replacement of the gospel with political agendas within Protestantism has caused the worry behind this conference. One reason that does not happen in Catholicism is that it has a recognized place for social teaching and a recognized way for deriving it. This prevents social teaching from becoming either totalitarian or free-floating in the life of the church. In the Protestant churches, there is no control over social teaching. An agenda simply grabs the center and gives itself out as Christian faith. That does not mean that the way Catholicism does it is necessarily the best way. But it's a better way than Protestantism's."

Lotz quickly added that there is a Protestant problem with social teaching because Protestantism tends to downplay reason that is not derived directly from the gospel. In fact, he suggested, reason, which can also be referred to as natural law, is usually left out of the Protestant social canon.

Brian Benestad did not want the conference to look at Roman Catholicism through rose-colored glasses, so he did what he could to remove them. "One has to ask whether Catholic social teaching and its policy proposals are crowding out teaching on faith and morals. There is a real religious illiteracy among Catholics these days. And yet what do the bishops do? They become identified with the peace pastoral or the economics pastoral and not with any kind of effort to do much about religious illiteracy or the basics of the faith. The bishops, when they make their policy statements, argue that they are speaking as pastors. But it seems to me that they are not really speaking as pastors. Indeed, they confuse themselves and others. They unleash a spirit of dissent. They encourage people to agree or disagree with their pastoral positions, but then that style naturally moves over to other areas, such as the traditional areas of faith and morals."

This struck a note with Ken Myers, who described a case of religious illiteracy outside the church. "When I worked for National Public Radio," he said, "I was once speaking with a reporter who had done some coverage of religion-and-politics issues. In passing I said something about the grace of God, and he said 'What?' Fortunately, he did not say 'Who?' This reporter held a masters degree in philosophy from a prestigious midwestern university, and in all of his academic work he had never encountered the concept of the grace of God. Obviously, he had not encountered it in his coverage of religious activism."

For the time being Neuhaus set aside the abstractions of the social teaching of the church and considered what actually happens to church documents once they are approved. "How are the bishops' statements used in the actual pedagogy and activism of the Roman Catholic community? In George Weigel's remarkable book *Tranquillitas Ordinis: The Present Failure and Future Promise of Roman Catholic Thought on War and Peace,* there is a long quotation from Bryan Hehir speaking to Network, which is an activist organization led mainly by a number of sisters. Bryan says the purpose of the church's teaching in the bishops' statements is to establish what he called a 'constituency of conscience' (a phrase once used by George McGovern) to develop a specific political direction, to enlist the institutional church to ratify that direction, and then to see how many people in the church can be recruited to it. It is an extraordinarily candid statement, for someone as nuanced as Father Hehir usually is, about what the overall pastoral strategy is with respect to what happens once the bishops have made their somewhat sophisticated distinctions about general principles, particular teachings, and prudential judgment— in other words, when they get thrown into the life of the church."

Tom Oden voiced similar concerns about the Protestant denominations and their implementation of social teachings. "There is a very subtle collusion," said Oden, "between church legislative assemblies and the institutional bureaucracies that implement the mandates of those assemblies. The texts of the social teaching documents are usually not so bad. But when you watch the implementation of them, something else occurs. They are written in equivocal language by the legislative assemblies that will look okay to a church body. But then it will be influenced by bureaucratic elites who often control the language, and it will be used in a highly programmatic way. This is especially true in the United Methodist Church. This sort of collusion tends to fit in with the New Class or knowledge class premise."

Thomas Hopko then intervened to bend the attention of the conference from the social teachings of the church to the social functions of the church. "There are very particular social-political functions that go beyond simple detached statements about principles,"

Hopko stated. "You can see this through history, regardless of the so-cial order that Christians lived in. There were many changes through history. There was a time when Christianity was illegal. When the emperor was killing Christians, Christian leadership said 'We are supposed to pray for him—not remove him from our prayer because he is killing us, but to pray for him.' The pastoral epistles and Romans 13 were written under that situation. Then you have the Constantinian era and the whole era of the monastic development. Then you have the imperial period, the Byzantine time. Then the time under Islam. Then in our time the national Christianities. In the midst of all that, there was always thinking about the place of the church—particularly the clergy—in the world. And always, in addi-tion to pronouncing principles and preaching gospel sermons about salvation, there are very particular social functions for the church."

Hopko listed and described the church's four main social func-tions as Orthodoxy sees them. "The first function of the church is to challenge the ultimacy of the political, to always say No. Politics is never totally right. It is never absolute. It can never be sanctioned by the gospel as such. In it there is always the element of error and sin, so you cannot identify the Christian faith with any public order. If the church aligns itself with one particular policy, it loses its ability to relativize all of them, to put a question mark behind all of them. That is what Jesus did. Jesus questioned all—the Zealots, the Sad-ducees, and so on, and he indicated that there is still something else. In actual practice it is very important that the church does this too.

"And it is very important for a second reason—namely, the mediation function. Because if you have to speak the gospel and to be the pastor to all the people and yet you align yourself with a cer-tain public policy, then the implication is that the others are ex-cluded—if not technically excommunicated because they cannot go to Holy Communion, then factually excommunicated from the going line of their own church. And that is a problem. One of the functions of the episcopate was to be the center of unity and to guarantee freedom of expression, for controversy, and for contrast to all. There is a kind of social duty there that becomes weakened, if not destroyed, by aligning the church even prudentially with one or another policy. That is why it cannot be done. But when it is done, and the church goes to the next step and says that if one does not do this then one is not a Christian, then you have apostasy.

"Third, the clergy and the bishops have not only to challenge and mediate, but also to engage in intercession and mediation before God, holding the whole thing before God. The area of prayer is very important. I was shocked by Professor Berger's example about the political act of the church not praying for the Führer. I don't think that intercession on behalf of the powers and holding the reality before God means that you agree with them. On the contrary, if you don't agree, you'd better pray harder. The church prays not just for one side or for one policy's success. Every time you pray, it has got to occur to you that you might be wrong. Therefore, prayer is relativizing by definition, because you hold it before God and say, 'Thy will be done,' thereby acknowledging that you may not be doing God's will. So the real practice of prayer in its political sense is very important.

"The fourth thing is prophecy, but in the technical sense of the term. You don't prophesy after you have heard experts address an issue for five years. There are situations where the preacher or the bishop will prophesy by saying, 'This is wrong, thus saith the Lord.' That is a direct inspiration of the Spirit. If that is part of what being baptized and receiving the Holy Spirit is for, then that will be a so-cial-political act. It cannot be programmed, but it will happen. Part of the problem is how you institutionalize prophecy. Well, you don't. When prophecy is done in history—for example, through the Confessing Church in Nazi Germany—it is never done purely in terms of a political position or a political party. It says that anyone who does something is wrong: if you kill people because they are Jews, it is wrong; if you claim that a black person is not human, it is wrong. Again, prophecy does not consist in consulting three experts and writing a paper. There has to be some kind of direct inspiration. That will be there all of the time."

Hopko's Orthodox contribution to the conference conversation was taken by the conferees to be orthodox indeed. Around the table there was much enthusiastic support for the social functions of the church as Hopko and Orthodoxy had laid them out. They appeared to bridge a rather wide Lutheran-Catholic gap on the issue of church social teaching.

To Discriminate or Not

The conference was organized under the basic assumption that the church should engage in what Reinhold Niebuhr called the indis-criminate criticism of society. That is, the church should place all societies—including their political arrangements, their economies, and their cultures—under the judgment of the kingdom of God. In that way the church finds that all societies, without exception, fall infinitely short of the coming kingdom.

Regarding the church's discriminating criticism of society—or more specifically, the way in which the church compares specific societies and their political economies and prudentially judges which are better and which worse—there was no consensus. Dannhauser raised the issue again: "I wonder if our discussion of the relation of the church and politics is not doomed to abstractness as long as we do not talk about differences in regimes. Take slavery for an example. It makes a world of difference if you are talking about slavery in one kind of society or slavery in another kind of society. Don't we demand of the church that it have some kind of teaching regarding some regimes being better than others? This does not mean that the church should say that liberal democracy is the only legitimate kind of regime. But don't we want the churches to say that tyranny is an impermissible regime? Do we really want a church that has no teaching on different regimes?"

Dulles replied that "that of course has been discussed much down through the centuries—whether the church should foster monarchy, aristocracy, democracy, or a balanced combination of all of them. On the whole, various kinds of regimes can be legitimate, as long as they are against tyranny—whether the tyranny of the individual or the tyranny of the mob. The church does have a position on this, but it is fairly tolerant of different kinds of regimes in different kinds of situations."

Lovelace then brought up the case of the Philippines, which at the time was very much in the news. He claimed that the Filipino base communities—which are small groups of Christians that gather for prayer, Bible study, and what is called "Christian praxis"—definitely made politically discriminating judgments against Marcos and company that markedly differed from those of the magisterium. Furthermore, Lovelace said that "a lot of us have the feeling that this is a kind of Psalm 2 event in history. This is an event where a very unrighteous government was toppled by the prayers of Christian believers."

Dulles then offered a correction to the Lovelace account: "It was not only the base communities that engaged the political order. It was also the hierarchy, the bishops themselves, who contested the legitimacy of the results of the Filipino election. Admittedly, with advice coming from the Vatican, an intramagisterial conflict developed. The local bishops said that they must do what they have to do in their local situation. The Vatican was more concerned with the long-term repercussions, what would happen to the church in Korea and Taiwan and so forth if the Philippines were taken as a precedent for other action. And we still have to see, for the results are not yet in. It may prove that it was a mistake."

Speaking as the political realist that he is, Berger challenged Lovelace: "President Marcos was not overthrown by prayer but by the United States deciding he was expendable and taking action in that direction. Anyone who is in favor of liberal democracy and who likes social change to be accompanied by as little bloodshed as possible will pray that Mrs. Aquino will succeed. She is a very attractive political leader, and the regime she is putting together has some very sensible policies. But we have no idea how this thing is going to end. An unspeakable disaster could be building up there, partly because Mrs. Aquino is rather incompetent. She is very attractive as a person, but she is politically incompetent. What then about this great action of the base communities? Again, we do not get brownie points for good intentions. We get brownie points in history for results."

Fortin decided not to comment on the Philippines, but he did line up with those who favored the church's attempting discriminating judgments. He asserted that the church cannot "just preach justice in the abstract. Justice always takes a particular form relative to a particular regime. It is aristocratic justice, or democratic justice, and so on." Neuhaus then recalled that Chesterton said there was no reform without form—which means, he suggested, that the church, which is forever seeking societal reform this side of the kingdom, will of necessity make discriminating judgments regarding politics, economics, and culture. Its judgments will be—or should be—interesting and distinctive, since they should flow from the life, the tradition, the integrity, and the normative truths of the Christian community. When the church's discriminating societal statements are cut off from its internal history, such statements become "damned uninteresting," Neuhaus said.

With this session of the conference drawing to a close, Avery Dulles sketched a consensus opinion that he sensed was emerging. The consensus, he said, affirmed that there are political or quasi-political ramifications of the gospel itself. He suggested wryly that even Peter Berger agreed with this. Also, the conferees generally agreed that the church, in principle, should oppose totalitarianism, slavery, genocide, and torture. And finally, they agreed that, because of unintended consequences and other problems, the church should be very cautious about applying its principles and teachings in society.

Then Dulles said, "The word *prophecy* is bandied around a little too loosely by many in our time. There are more false prophets than true prophets in the world. The fact that a person is prophetic does not give me any great confidence in what he or she is saying.

"The gospel certainly gives us a sense of reverence and respect and love for the poor. It does not permit us to write them off as non-persons. That is extremely important, and it must be said again and again. And you can say that Jesus does have a certain bias toward the poor. But Jesus does not take up the cause of those who suffer religious or social discrimination. It is one of those things which we think Jesus ought to have done, but he did not do it. He showed a great deal of mercy and love to the poor, but he never took up their *cause* in the sense in which that word is understood today. He didn't encourage the poor to rise up, nor did he demand a new social order."

Dulles seemed to be saying that the presence of false prophecy does not take away the need for authentic prophecy, that the fact that there are some who politicize poverty does not take away the church's responsibility to be with and care for the poor, and that bad discriminating judgments do not take away the church's duty to judge societies and situations in an intelligently discriminating way. His Catholic perspective definitely emphasized law and social teaching.

THE PROTESTANT PROPOSAL

Up to now the conference had examined the alleged apostasy of American Protestantism from three perspectives—the perspectives of sociology, history, and Catholic theology. Now a Protestant theologian would focus his sights on the perceived problem in American Protestantism and offer a proposal for theological reconstruction and for the ordering of life, temporal and eternal.

The theologian of the hour was Robert Jenson of St. Olaf College. "I have chosen to concentrate on the theological problem posed by what I take to be the occasioning phenomenon of this conference," he began. "American Protestantism, through large tracts of its life, has undertaken to order temporal life—both its own and, not content with that, the life of the world at large—otherwise than by ordering from its own God. I take it that that is the unbelief referred to in the call to this conference. And I take it that that is the apostasy referred to in Peter Berger's paper.

"Is it really correct to say that secular or alien agendas, political or otherwise, have pushed their way into the place in the church which belongs to God's revelation? Or, have they been sucked into that place? It seems to me that the latter is the case. What makes that fairly plain to me is that almost any alien agenda will do. This conference concentrates on political agendas, but therapeutic agendas are probably more common occupants of the place of divine revelation within Protestantism than political agendas. It seems to me fairly plain from the phenomenon that we observe that God's revelation has already vacated the heart of the church, so all of these other things rush in. They are sucked in to fill the vacuum." The solution, Jenson suggested, lies in filling the vacuum that now attracts the alien agendas.

But before he tried to fill the vacuum, Jenson stepped back to gain a little perspective on the American Protestant problem today: "I regard the efforts of Western Christianity since about 1780 as the effort to overcome the Enlightenment, as it used to be put in Germany. Not in the sense of eliminating it, but in the sense of dealing creatively with it. The particular history of American Christianity is determined by that effort in a very specific sense: the relationship of both the American nation and the American church to the Enlightenment is a very special one, different from that which any nation or church in Europe can conceivably have, because in a real sense America was the nation invented by the Enlightenment. And the dominant forms of Christianity in this country are brought to this country by the same groups that were the enlighteners of Europe.

"Let me state the schema of my proposal: the synthesis of understanding and inclination in which the ordering of human life occurs is, in Christianity, enabled by Christianity's specific interpretation of God; and the doctrine of the Trinity is the fruit, to date, of Christianity's attempts to identify and interpret the one and only God. The synthesis of understanding and inclination in which the ordering of anybody's life consists is, in Christianity, established by its specific interpretation of God. When the latter fails, so must the former. But of course when that happens the church will not cease to be concerned for order—its own order and that of society; it will only have to carry out that concern by alien and inappropriate means. The next step in the schema: the triune interpretation of God was never quite finished in Western Christianity. Now, the next suggestion in the schema: in the history of Western Christianity it has been the institution of the church that has filled the gap left by the incomplete Christian doctrine of God. When Protestantism both abhors the church on the one hand and fails to take up the trinitarian task on the other, a disordering of its life is the inevitable result. If one asks what we are to do about it, I guess my answer is that we ought not to attempt to improve our understanding of civil society, as if that could be done as an autonomous enterprise; rather, we should think together more profoundly about the identity and reality of the God we worship."

Neuhaus commented that Roman Catholicism was fortunate,

for when its theology fell weak, its ecclesiology acted as a substitute of sorts. Unfortunately, Protestantism does not have an ecclesiology that is sturdy enough to be called into play. It might not even possess enough theological substance to make possible a theological retrieval or recovery like the one Oden was suggesting.

Jenson agreed: "If one can operate momentarily with Paul Tillich's famous distinction between Catholic substance and Protestant principle, I think there is a real possibility that the substance has been so gnawed at by American Protestantism that its retrieval is unlikely."

Is Doctrinal Tinkering Enough?

Peter Berger both criticized and cheered the Jenson proposal. His criticism came first, as criticism often does: "What troubles me about the paper is the underlying assumption about the relation of ideas and history. I was reminded of Alasdair MacIntyre's book *After Virtue.* According to MacIntyre, all our troubles are due to a couple of philosophical mistakes that were made in the Middle Ages, and we have to correct them. Now Jenson also points out a couple of mistakes that were made. The Eastern trinitarian tradition arrived in the West in damaged form. Unfortunately, an opportunity that Jonathan Edwards had was not taken up by American Protestantism, and so on. In other words, the gist of the trouble is that a number of intellectual mistakes were made and that we now have to correct them and that will solve our problems. I have problems with that. I would not for a moment underestimate the role of ideas in history, but I do not think that history is moved in that way. The image I get is that Professor Jenson basically agrees with my diagnosis of the problem of the church today but somehow he thinks the solution is going to come out of a series of theological commissions that will rectify these mistakes. That troubles me."

Berger concluded his critique by asking how the theological enterprise in which Jenson was laboring might be related or conveyed to the life of the church. The sociologist went on to suggest that preaching might be the key.

Then Berger praised the Jenson project: "What I like very much about the paper—and this paradoxically is close to what troubles me—is that Jenson is doing theology. For me, as a social scientist, it is absolutely wonderful to encounter theologians who do theology—instead of sociology. I can learn something from them. I cannot learn anything from all this stuff where people tell me what society is like in the name of God."

Jenson answered the criticism, "Well, where would the ideas that I proposed be effective? I think they would be effective in the life of the church. That is why I suggest at the end of my paper that the reform needed is a liturgical and a homiletical reform. I don't think that one can do anything about urging on a direct confrontation with the living God. That is up to him. We cannot reform the church to have more confrontations with the living God—but we can reform it liturgically and homiletically. The locus of a radicalized trinitarianism in the life of the Protestant church is precisely a liturgical life that has got a trinitarian shape to it. Protestantism, by and large, does not have and has not had this for a long time.

"Protestants in worship usually hear prayers addressed to God the Father, sing hymns from revivalist antecedents, and then hear a long discourse," Jenson asserted, noting further that this had been brought home to him recently when he suggested to a group of Lutheran pastors that they enter a properly trinitarian anaphora into the liturgy. They replied by asking what difference that would make. Jenson supposed that this nonchalant attitude toward trinitarian worship probably pervades American Protestantism. Nontrinitarian worship sharply contrasts with "the trinitarian shape of Christian worship, which is above all exemplified in the very structure of the eucharist. The way that piece of theater is put together reveals the triune God. Worship so structured is triune in its dramatic character."

Neuhaus then responded to Jenson's thesis: "When Christians are no longer excited about God, they get excited about a lot of other things—therapeutic agendas, political agendas, institutional power games, and so forth. Some Christians are no longer excited about God because they had such a thin doctrine of God that they wore it out. They just got weary of it. Their doctrine of God was not exciting enough to contain their religious energy, and so their religious energy moved away from contemplation of God and engagement in the life of God to engagement in something else that looked exciting—politics, changing the world, or whatever."

"That does not quite get it," said Jenson, "though what you have said is also true. I think the problem is more specific than that. Like Edwards said, it really is a specific relationship of time and eternity, constituted in the triunity of God, that orders human life. To use Edwards again, it brings together affection, knowledge, and inclination. So, even the most powerful, most interesting doctrine of God, if it were effectively unitarian—as I would suggest the doctrine of God in Protestant Christianity is—would still not do for Christians what needs to be done. It still would not order their lives."

Dannhauser followed by reminding the group of the James Turner thesis—that modern atheism in America is an inside job—that is, it is a demolition job on the doctrine of God that was done inside the church. Then he surprised his listeners by arguing that "that has to do with the overarticulation of the doctrine of the Trinity and an excess of theology and systematic theology. What lends plausibility to that is that Islam and Judaism, though they have a lot of problems of their own, were left relatively untouched by the death-of-God theology. As they might have said, 'Our God did not die because he was not alive in the same sense. We never attempted to say that much about him. We concentrated on the law rather than theology.' So one could say that theology is part of the disease, not the cure."

Focusing the conference on the human experience of the Trinity, Richard Lovelace said, "In one of the documents connected with the National Council of Churches' apostolic faith study with the filioque clause, Leslie Newbigin is quoted as saying that in most of Western Christianity we are creedally trinitarian but functionally unitarian in our living. That is powerfully true. So I appreciate Professor Jenson's paper—especially since any friend of Edwards is a friend of mine. But what Edwards seems to be saying is this: in order to comprehend what can be known about God, we need a divine and supernatural light, we need the illuminating work of the Holy Spirit in us. This epistemological function of the Holy Spirit is crucial. It looks to me as if we need a powerful infusion of the Holy Spirit in order to do theology or to be enabled to order our lives. If Edwards were sitting here he would say, 'Don't tinker with your doctrine. Pray for a greater effusion of the Spirit.' The problem may not be so much theological doctrine as it is our actual personal experience of both the Son and the Spirit. We do not cultivate our relationship to either."

Jenson was not unsympathetic to Lovelace's concern for experience of the Trinity. So Lovelace rhetorically asked if the proposed liturgical and homiletical reform would "mean that what one most does with regard to the Spirit is pray for his appearance and his outpouring?" Jenson then answered emphatically: "Of course that is what it means. What is of decisive significance is prayer for the Spirit's coming."

Hopko mentioned that Jenson's connection between the life of the Trinity and the ordering of society is not so farfetched. It has surfaced before. For example, Hopko said, "A strange Russian, who both Tolstoy and Dostoyevski thought was a genius and a saint, wrote a huge two-volume work called *The Philosophy of the Common*

Task about the ordering of political life. The epigraph of the work is 'The Trinity, Our Social Program.'"

Hopko agreed with Lovelace that doctrinal reform and reformulation are necessary but not sufficient for the reordering of life. "The issue is not so much speculative theology about the Trinity," contended Hopko. "It is about the trinitarian character of the ecclesial community as a kind of a model for the polis. Ordering our life in the ecclesial and political categories rather than the temporal and eternal categories might be another way of formulating the issue. There is a tradition which would say that whatever the theologians are writing, there is a worshipping church where there is the one God, the Word of God, and the breath of God. But the entrance into that life comes through worship, not through theological speculation. Because the speculation comes through the worship. Therefore, the proper ordering of relations between human beings and God and among human beings is taken from the trinitarian relation. But where that is lived out is in the ecclesial community, incarnate as worship. The Roman Catholics at least still have the eucharist and the mass and the gathering of the church as a sacramental institution incarnate in space and time, where theologians come and go, and where prayer is through the Word to the Father in the Spirit. That particular experience as a eucharistic community has something to say about how we ought to order our life in this world. That is the key."

Jenson responded with an academic amen: "Theological fine-tuning is perfectly meaningless unless what is being fine-tuned is the liturgy and preaching. Then, the relevance of trinitarian theology is that if God is triune and if he is the Creator, then a movement of trinitarian insight in the life of the church simply means a firmer grasp on reality, as the gospel reveals it. This includes our societal reality as well. The life of the church, to be rightly ordered in itself, must be triunely ordered. It should be possible to derive from the church a certain understanding of the essential character of human community, from which understanding some political judgments could indeed be made. They could, for example, have more to say about totalitarianism than simply that it is awful. For there are not many people who think it isn't. Not even Lenin thought it was nice; he just thought it was necessary. But why is it awful?" A triunely ordered church might suggest answers to that question, said Jenson.

After politely listening to a suggestion or two that Jenson's paper tended to encourage a kind of unhelpful theological speculation and abstraction, the Chicago Lutheran Carl Braaten came to the defense of the St. Olaf Lutheran. "I understand Dr. Jenson's paper to be an attack on speculation, because he wants the gospel, which communicates the very being of God, to be sufficient for us. It is a radical summons of obedience to the gospel, not an invitation to speculation." Jenson could not have asked for a stronger defense. By then all around the table were convinced that Jenson was after far more than a little theological tinkering.

Reforming the Reformation

Neuhaus set forth a couple of questions that shaped the remainder of the conference. "In the life of the church how can the only reformation that makes sense to me, that is worthy of the name reformation, take place? And how can people be excited again by God?" He proceeded to clarify his questions.

First, he wanted to make it clear that he was not calling for a follow-up to the 1975 Hartford Appeal. Second, he insisted that the questions should not be interpreted in any way as suggesting that "if the church were once again excited about God and about participating in the life of the Holy Trinity that this would diminish its sense of responsibility for the right ordering of the world or for politics or for social change. I think, in fact, that a renewed church might be even more politically engaged, but it would be an engagement with a difference. It would visibly and believably be ordered 'from God,' as Professor Jenson is suggesting. That is, the manner of engagement would be ordered from God, rather than ordered from some alien source."

The best guess of Ken Myers was that the renewal of the church would be related to a rediscovery of the holiness of God. That rediscovery, stipulated Myers, would go beyond the evangelical tendency to reduce holiness to morality.

Speaking as an evangelical, Lovelace returned to the necessity of experiencing God. "Again," he said, "if Jonathan Edwards were here, he would very strongly say, 'Only the Holy Spirit, only God at his initiative, can get us excited and can illuminate us properly about himself.' Of course the question is, What can we do from our side to open ourselves to the divine initiative, to bring God around to this renewing work? I have written two books about that. At the moment I am rejoicing that there is much interest in spiritual theology today. We do have more books coming out on that that are not simply relational froth. Some of them stress the recovery of the classical disciplines, which essentially mean 'Slow down and pay attention to God.' There is a resurgence of concern for spiritual renewal that is theologically well grounded." Lovelace was particularly heartened that there are seminaries—namely, Princeton and Andover Newton—that seem headed toward postmodern orthodoxies, though the vitalities at such places are very disordered.

Stallsworth was quick to reinforce the point made by Lovelace. "I do wonder where the reformation of American Christianity might come from. Admittedly, I have a pastoral approach and I come from a church with a revivalistic heritage, the United Methodist Church. But I would guess that reformation will probably come, if it is to come at all, from an encounter with the living God. Now the living God is trinitarian—Father, Son, and Holy Spirit. But still, that encounter, that engagement, is crucial, absolutely essential. It is essential to be able to say, 'Yes, I have encountered this God. Yes, the church is encountering this God.' That encounter always involves crisis, the crisis of grace and judgment. Not one sector of the church can say that it can escape that crisis or that it is going to bring on this crisis by its own work. The whole church experiences it.

"Too often today there is something similar to a sociological aloofness in the doing of theology," Stallsworth continued. "Now that perspective has its place and its benefits, to be sure. The sociologist, as Peter Berger would argue, stands above the fray, examining and analyzing the social movements of the moment. But this same type of aloofness seems to have come to the theologians. There is a doctrinal aloofness in which we talk about tinkering with this doctrine or that, or changing this emphasis, or 'reprioritizing.' There seems to be an escape from the necessity and the reality of encountering the living and trinitarian God." Not all of the Lutherans present were edgy about these expressions of religious "enthusiasm," for Carl Braaten later extended and deepened Stallsworth's concerns about "theological aloofness."

Dulles contended that the crux of today's problem is community, or the lack of it: "The problem of talking about God is very closely related to the lack of a community of discourse in which God-language can be meaningful. And that is very closely related to the collapse of the church as a real and genuine community. Now, the parish or congregation that comes together on Sunday really is not a community. It is a collection of individuals who come together only for an hour a week and have very little in common. What constitutes the basics of their thinking is mostly what they have in common—television and newspapers, which are secular and which do not tolerate meaningful theological language. Specifically Christian concerns are bracketed in order to enter into the media of discourse. Where religious language is revitalized and people get concerned about theological things is where you have a relatively autonomous community. Take, for example, charismatic and covenant communities where the members talk to and educate each other over a fairly long period of time in some degree of isolation from the general society. Remember the kinds of things that Bonhoeffer said about the German secular universities of his time—where doctrine cannot be taken seriously, there the gospel and worship cannot be taken seriously. He had to put all of his hope in certain seminaries. I think this is the kind of situation we might be in in the United States today. That is not a very optimistic statement, I am afraid." This was a rather solemn appraisal from one whose church is alleged to possess an ecclesiology that will get it through theologically thin times.

Several others picked up the theme of the church and what it ought to be up to. Glenn Tinder was among them: "I have a couple of suggestions for the life of the church. One is suffering. When I think about the lives that Americans now live, under the welfare state and under consumer capitalism, and when I consider how shameful Americans consider suffering to be, I feel that the cross really has no place in this society. But it surely is relevant to the church and to us that the life of Christ came out of suffering and death. The whole idea that new life will come to the gospel and to the church and to us as Christians through suffering needs to be considered.

"The second thought is connected with politics. It is about love. During this conference we have not said very much about love, though it has been implicit in a lot of things we have had to say. In 1 John it is written that he who does not love does not know God, for God is love. Somehow it is love which is essential for providing access to God. This of course does not mean love without theological substance, or love without reforming the liturgy, or love isolated from other things. If one could apply St. Paul's 1 Corinthians 13 here, theology, reform of the liturgy, and all of these things are nothing without love. While love is primarily a face-to-face relationship, love for the neighbor, love also unfolds in and necessarily has repercussions for the political world."

Without hesitation Hopko concurred with Tinder that love is crucial to the church, but he also wanted to nail down a more precise definition of Christian love. After all, Hopko said, the political and psychological gospels going around these days have their own definitions and applications of what they call "love." "If God is love, then the revelation of God in Christ is not only the revelation of God but also the revelation of what love really is. In Christ we see what love is. It is not a smiling face. It is the God who crucifies his Son, who smashes the vessels, who prunes the vines, who beats the children, who wounds the lover. This is love. Sentimentalized love and romanticized love are easy uses of the word *love*. When we say 'God' or 'love,' we should not assume that people know what we are talking about. That is at the very center of today's problem." In the church, Hopko concluded, to speak of love is to speak of the Trinity and of the Trinity's second person, who is crucified outside the gates of the polis.

Turner continued to hold the conference's attention on the church and, more specifically, the typical Roman Catholic parish. "Speaking as a Roman Catholic layperson, I can see that a lot of the life of the church is shared with the life of the laity. The bishops talk to us about nuclear war. And I do not mind that, though I may or may not agree with what they say about nuclear war. Liturgical change, in one way or another, brings in the laity. Recently when the bishops were considering the status of women there was an attempt to bring the laity in. And at the parish level we have groups for prayer, for Bible study (though not in the technical sense), for social action, for liturgy."

Then, agreeing with an earlier comment by Neuhaus, the Michigan historian noted, "One thing we do not have, one thing that is not shared with us, is theological reflection. I would not want to privilege theological reflection above prayer or the liturgy, because I do not think it should be privileged. It is a secondary activity. But it does seem that theological reflection can deepen prayer and worship. One of the reasons the life of the church in areas other than the political seems thin, unappealing, and possibly boring is that at the level of the laity we have an increasingly thin sense of God and the Trinity and most other facts which are at the center of our religious existence. If there is one thing that should be done in a practical way to reestablish and strengthen the primacy of the gospel, it might be theological reflection at the parish level."

Steinfels greeted Turner's statement with enthusiastic assent. Furthermore, she contended that the language now employed by the theologians of the church tends to be esoteric and private and that what the church needs is a more public language. This, she suggested, would increase lay knowledge of Roman Catholicism's theological enterprise.

Here Stallsworth noted what he thought to be an interesting development: "The locus of a possible reformation might be changing from the seminary or university to the local church. When we are talking about liturgical reform, we are talking about the local church. When we talk about the community loving and suffering, we are talking about the local church. When we talk about renewed standards of Christian theological education among the laity, again we are talking about the local church. Reformation in the past—for example, the Lutheran case—has oftentimes been connected with the university and the seminary. But I think a shift might be in the wind."

Oden was not content to mention one or two sources of renewal. He had six sources on hand and he listed them: "Pray for the outpouring of the Holy Spirit. Be ready to suffer death for the gospel, to share in Christ's suffering. Defend the orthodox faith. Order life sacramentally in a holistic way. Be justified by grace through faith alone. And develop disciplined, nurturing communities that would manifest and embody the life of faith." Those six visions of renewal, Oden explained, "are attached to six different centuries in which there were significant reformations of the Christian community. We see the question of the renewal of the Christian community from some locus, some historical memory. The question we are responding to was framed by Pastor Neuhaus in a sixteenth-century, Reformation way. That is one way to frame it, one very significant way to frame it. But there are other ways to frame it. For example, from the second-century point of view, learning how to suffer and take risks. From the fourth century, learning how to articulate and defend the orthodox faith and to relate it to the polis. Here I am thinking of the Constantinian period. From the thirteenth century I am thinking about the sacramental life that was manifest in medieval Scholastic thinking. From the sixteenth century the reformation focused on justification. From the eighteenth century the Wesleyan ethos, in which you have a highly intentional process of nurturing—small, primary communities. But the sixth point comes out of nineteenth-century revivalism. It may be our greatest need: prayer. That was Finney's first point in the nurturing of revival. And it saturated the language of revival: pray for the outpouring of the Holy Spirit. We do not know how to do that in the church very well."

Reformation and Campus

Werner Dannhauser brought higher education into the conversation. Biblical illiteracy, according to Dannhauser, is the real demon today. To illustrate his point he reported that in his many years of teaching the Bible in the Great Books series, only once had he encountered a student who knew the Bible better than he. So, the renewal of the Christian community, he believed, will certainly be bound up with increasing knowledge of the Old and New Testaments. This knowledge will come in part from educators getting students to read the Bible.

Benestad of Scranton also advocated more knowledge: "Once we have the knowledge of who God is and what he has done, we can be grateful. But we do not know that, so we are not that grateful. For example, the other day in class we were talking about liberation from sin and how that is one of the great things that God has done for us. The students were not that excited about it, because they do not have much of a sense that they have committed sin and that they need liberation." If a basic knowledge of God were broadened and deepened among the laity, and if the discipline of moral theology were recharged, said Benestad, the chances for a reformation of the church would be greatly enhanced.

It is no wonder that today's college students know little about the Bible and little about God, asserted Arthur Holmes of Wheaton College. Most of them are all wrapped up in a subjectivist version of Christianity, the anti-intellectualism of popular culture, job-getting, and careerism. According to Holmes, this leads students to compartmentalize their thinking about God. "But we have to decompartmentalize our thinking about God. We have to think Christianly about everything. We have to impart that sense of the presence of God to all areas of thought and all areas of life. This sort of thinking applies outside academia as well." Holmes reported that he had detected a distinct hunger for such theological decompartmentalization while teaching a series of lessons entitled "God, the Creator of Heaven and Earth" in a mainline church.

Ernest Fortin took a minute to remind the conferees of the crisis in the church. "The case has been blown wide open. There is no orthodoxy anymore. This is the first time in history in which there is no single opinion that dominates anywhere. There are different groups holding different opinions, but where is orthodoxy today? The church has continued to uphold certain teachings, but how effective is that? What is persuasive? I don't mean to sound like an alarmist, but where do we begin? I would look at the schools and see what can be done within them—higher education, universities and seminaries. There is usually a trickle-down effect; sooner or later what starts out in higher education reaches the kiddies in the street."

If you do not believe in an academic trickle-down effect, Fortin smiled, listen to this story: "While I was attending a conference recently, I watched a little Saturday morning television. Usually I do not watch much TV, and never on Saturday morning. But in the hotel room I watched a cartoon for kiddies. In the cartoon two little girls were shown in the backyard somewhere and out of the hedge jumped this huge animal. One of the little girls says, 'Gee, that's scary.' The other little girl said, 'Scary is a value judgment.' Here is modern social science coloring the judgment of five-year-olds." By now several had joined the cartoon-watcher in his snickering.

Then the good professor from Boston College described an imaginative way to use the trickle-down effect for the good: "On the campus you might try to get groups of people together and interested in significant ideas. Others, seeing this, might become curious and ask questions that had not occurred to them before. This is happening at Boston College. We organized a little program with lectures and seminars regularly attended by fifty or sixty people, a group much larger than we anticipated. Every time we hold a session others come in because they've heard about it or because they're interested in the subject. What strikes them is the fact that students are engrossed in what the speaker is saying and that they carry on a discussion with him for an hour and a half afterward. There is so much debonair nihilism on campus, in which students aren't for anything and they aren't against anything. We can use this opportunity to get them interested. That could attract them."

David Lotz described and then prescribed. "There has been a proliferation of gospels. There are gospels everywhere. Though we have been concentrating on political gospels, the therapeutic is also triumphing. Because gospels are everywhere, that has cheapened *the* gospel as well as replaced it. The same thing obtains with regard to our language about God. It is not that we are not talking about God. God is being talked about constantly in virtually every theological context. God-language is invoked again and again to explain virtually everything that is happening in the world. What we are suffering from is an extreme instrumentalism. God-language is used as a way to talk about something else. We need more linguistic chastening and modesty. The divine name should not be uttered so lightly."

Then Lotz spoke about the contemporary seminary scene: "In the Protestant seminaries there is now no spiritual formation. That has evacuated our understanding of God. Today there is a need in seminaries to restore the centrality of spiritual formation, for the sake of those who are to form others into the body of Christ and into the image of Christ."

Said Neuhaus, "So, you want to restore God to God-talk, and you want the seminaries to stop producing smart unbelievers and also smart-aleck unbelievers."

Carl Peter was one who was not chuckling, for he was not entirely taken by Lotz's plea for less God-talk. Peter said there are some contemporary church and academic circles that could stand some more talk about the Almighty. "I am convinced that it would be helpful for the church to take the mandate of 1 Peter a little more seriously: 'In your hearts reverence Christ as Lord. Always be prepared to make a defense to any one who calls you'—and here I would gloss: or is even vaguely interested—'to account for the hope that is yours.'"

Braaten went with the drift of Peter's comment. First he realistically framed the group's task: "Not one of us can bring about the reformation. So we have to start more modestly, and ask the question, 'What can we as teachers, as theologians, as academicians do?"

Then Braaten boldly pointed to the theological problem in the seminaries: "Probably the major divinity schools are already into the abyss. They have gone over the line. They are probably irretrievable. Maybe that is too much of a generalization. But it is definitely true at the University of Chicago. There is a divinity school there, but it does not teach theology. It teaches *about* theology, but it does not teach theology. It teaches *about* everybody else's theology, *about* systematic theology, *about* historical theology, but it does not teach theology. It is not a professing theology. The 'Here I stand,' the apologetic statement of the truth, in which the professor is so involved that his own theology is on the line in class after class, is absent. It is not happening, at least I don't think it's happening. So we have to take responsibility for the truth of theology. Theology really has to find a different kind of model than the academic model."

Braaten saw the same problem in academic associations: "No theology happens at the meetings at the American Academy of Religion. Three thousand people come together around religious subject matter. But honest to God, it is true that no theology happens, at least in my experience, year after year. So theology really does not flourish, particularly in those circles committed to the scientific study of religious phenomena. Theology does not happen in that academic setting. In fact, it cannot happen in a pluralistic situation. Maybe the church is the only context in the modern world in which real theology can take place."

But even in the churches theology must fight for its life. Braaten continued his indictment: "In Lutheranism we talk about politics. We talk about who is going to be elected bishop. We talk about how the church is restructuring itself. For example, at a recent convention of the Lutheran Church in America, nothing was said theologically in that five-day meeting. I was a delegate, so I know. I heard all kinds of other things being talked about and debated on the floor with a tremendous amount of passion and commitment. There is no shortage of that. But I had a strong sense that this is not an assembly of people committed to the gospel. They seemed ashamed to talk about the gospel. There is love and concern for people, but I think that people are ashamed of the gospel and feel awkward talking about it."

And even at the level of the local church, theology seems to be an endangered species, said Braaten. "Last week I was at an evangelism conference in northeastern Pennsylvania. Five ministers were asked to give statements about why their churches were growing, so that everybody else could take cues from them. The unexamined assumptions are that the living church is a growing church and that the evidences of growth are obvious. All the pastors spoke about what they are doing to make their churches grow, and of course everybody else was envious. One layman at the end of the conference got up and said, 'Am I way off the wall? Am I way out of line? I have not heard any of you pastors say anything about the gospel, anything about what you are really supposed to be doing. All you are talking about is recruiting church members.'

"So what can we do?" Braaten asked. His prescription was brief but very significant: "I think we have to press the case of the truth of Christianity, the kind of truth for which we are willing to lay down our lives. That kind of passion and commitment should be coupled with a sense that the time is very short."

Richard John Neuhaus, who had acted as moderator throughout the conference, concluded the conference with a summary of the proceedings that was definitely not abstractly academic: "I agree with Peter Berger's indictment. I think other gospels have pervasively displaced the gospel. James Turner demonstrated how historically this problem has happened again and again—that is, how people have attempted to keep the Christian enterprise going by reference to other gospels. Avery Dulles and the discussion his paper prompted went far beyond the Hartford Appeal. At Hartford, we were very carefully not confessional. I don't want to retract Hartford in any way. Hartford was right and abidingly important in what it said about transcendence and so forth. But the thrust of Dulles, Jenson, and this conference has been that unless the Christian community is able to order its life from God, as Professor Jenson puts it, that polis, the city of God in time, is not going to have much influence on the city of man. In fact, it won't have much to say. The church won't have anything substantive to say unless it represents some kind of right ordering that provokes the world to ask for reasons for the hope that is within us."

After taking Neuhaus's summary as a challenge, the conferees exchanged pleasantries, gathered up their belongings, and entered the bitter cold of that winter day in New York. Probably many of them were already busy formulating, with renewed vitality, the reasons for the hope that Neuhaus had referred to. The churches in America—or large sectors of the churches—are anxious to hear those reasons again. And it might be that such a hearing will begin to order the churches in such a way that they will contribute distinctively to the good ordering of society. That is a secondary hope, but a hope nonetheless.

Participants

J. Brian Benestad
Department of Theology and
    Religious Studies
University of Scranton

Peter L. Berger
Institute for the Study of
    Economic Culture
Boston University

Carl E. Braaten
Lutheran School of Theology at
    Chicago

Allan C. Carlson
The Rockford Institute

Werner J. Dannhauser
Department of Government
Cornell University

Avery Dulles, S.J.
School of Religious Studies
Department of Theology
Catholic University of America

Ernest L. Fortin
Department of Theology
Boston College

Arthur F. Holmes
Department of Philosophy
Wheaton College

Thomas Hopko
St. Vladimir's Orthodox
    Theological Seminary

Robert W. Jenson
St. Olaf College

David Lotz
Union Theological Seminary

Richard Lovelace
Gordon-Conwell Theological
    Seminary

Kenneth A. Myers
Formerly of *This World*

Richard John Neuhaus
The Rockford Institute
Center on Religion & Society

Thomas C. Oden
Theological School
Drew University

Carl J. Peter
Department of Theology
School of Religious Studies
Catholic University of America

Paul T. Stallsworth
The Rockford Institute
Center on Religion & Society

Margaret Steinfels
Commonweal

Glenn Tinder
University of Massachusetts—
    Boston

James Turner
Department of History
University of Michigan